Time isn't money; it's something of far mo̶ the case that we ought to be protecting our t product other resources. And best of all, he ̶

David Burkus, author of *U̶*

Steve Glaveski offers countless ways to get more out of each day by being Time Rich.

**Nir Eyal, best-selling author of
Hooked and *Indistractable***

Time Rich by Steve Glaveski makes a compelling argument for abandoning the archaic historical artefact of an 8 hour work-day (or any other arbitrary sum of time) as outmoded and irrelevant to the way we live and do our best work today. Glaveski offers both big ideas and specific techniques to contain or eliminate such time-snatching demons as meetings, email and social media. Reclaim the value of your time by forsaking the management of it and learning instead to manage energy, efficiency and attention — inputs with far greater impact on output and outcomes, not to mention quality of life.

**Whitney Johnson, award-winning author of
Disrupt Yourself and *Build an A-Team***

Time Rich is a fascinating look into why we're all so 'busy' — and how to gain back our most precious resource. Whether you're a beginner or a seasoned productivity geek, this book will change your life.

**Jonathan Levi, author, podcaster, and founder
of SuperHuman Academy**

A very worthwhile read for ambitious professionals to achieve that elusive work-life holy grail: being present and engaged at home without sacrificing anything on the work front — and even, perhaps, becoming more productive than you ever thought you could be.

**Andy Molinsky, award-winning author
of *Global Dexterity* and *Reach***

TIME
RICH

STEVE GLAVESKI

TIME
RICH

**DO YOUR BEST WORK,
LIVE YOUR BEST LIFE**

WILEY

First published in 2020 by John Wiley & Sons Australia, Ltd

42 McDougall St, Milton Qld 4064

Office also in Melbourne

Typeset in Cardea OTCE Reg 11/14pt

© John Wiley & Sons Australia, Ltd 2020

The moral rights of the author have been asserted

ISBN: 978-0-730-38387-1

A catalogue record for this book is available from the National Library of Australia

Cover design by Wiley

Cover image © doyz86 / Shutterstock

SKY25523D2B-63B7-4E11-AC8B-029D943FB876_101920

Disclaimer

The material in this publication is of the nature of general comment only, and does not represent professional advice. It is not intended to provide specific guidance for particular circumstances and it should not be relied on as the basis for any decision to take action or not take action on any matter which it covers. Readers should obtain professional advice where appropriate, before making any such decision. To the maximum extent permitted by law, the author and publisher disclaim all responsibility and liability to any person, arising directly or indirectly from any person taking or not taking action based on the information in this publication.

Contents

About the author

Steve Glaveski is on a mission to unlock the latent potential of people to create more impact for the world and lead more fulfilling lives.

Steve is the CEO of Collective Campus, a corporate innovation and startup accelerator that works with large organisations from Melbourne to Manila, and London to New York, to help better navigate change and uncertainty.

Collective Campus has worked with numerous heavyweights around the world, including Telstra, National Australia Bank, Clifford Chance, King & Wood Mallesons, BNP Paribas, Microsoft, Fox Sports, Village Roadshow, NTUC, Lufthansa, Bank of New Zealand, Ayala, OZ Minerals, Charter Hall, Maddocks, Mills Oakley, Australian Unity, Ascendas-Singbridge, Singapore Pools and MetLife, among others.

Collective Campus has incubated and been home to more than 100 startups, which have raised more than US$25 million between them. CC has also spun off a seed stage investment firm called Collective Venture Capital, which has invested in the likes of Konkrete and Ergogenic Health.

Aside from working with startups and large industry incumbents, Steve founded Lemonade Stand, a children's entrepreneurship program, and now SaaS platform that teaches children and teenagers the fundamentals of entrepreneurial thinking and doing. He also wrote the associated children's picture book, *Lemonade Stand: From Idea to Entrepreneur.*

Steve's other works include *The Innovation Manager's Handbook*, a self-published Amazon bestseller across a number of its categories, including startups, management and technology.

Steve hosts the award-winning *Future Squared* podcast, which at the time of writing was more than 370 episodes strong, having interviewed the likes of Adam Grant, Kevin Kelly, Gretchen Rubin, Marc Randolph, Tyler Cowen, and many more luminaries in their respective fields. The podcast earned the 2017 Popular Vote in the Business, Marketing & Entrepreneurship category in the inaugural Australian Podcast Awards People's Choice award.

Steve previously founded the office-sharing platform Hotdesk and has worked for the likes of Westpac, Dun & Bradstreet, the Victorian Auditor-General's Office, EY (formerly Ernst & Young), KPMG and Macquarie Bank.

His work has been featured in *Harvard Business Review*, *The Wall Street Journal*, *Forbes*, *The Australian Financial Review*, *Tech in Asia* and other outlets.

When he's not trying to help people unleash their potential, he can be found at the squat rack, skateboarding, surfing, on his motorcycle, hiking, catching a live band or with his head buried in a good book.

Acknowledgements

Thanks goes out to ...

- my team and extended family at Collective Campus and Lemonade Stand, without whose support I would struggle to live the time rich life that I lead
- all of our clients, startups and partners, without whose belief and support we would cease to operate
- my parents, without whose unrelenting and tireless work I would not have had the opportunity to build a life around writing books, hosting podcasts and doing work that fills me with joy for a living
- my family, my loved ones and my friends, both old and new — that includes one Jimmy Boskovski, whose name I regretfully and accidentally left out of the acknowledgements in my last book (here you go mate!)
- all of my *Future Squared* podcast guests and listeners
- all of the podcast hosts who have taken the time to have me on their shows
- Lucy Raymond, Chris Shorten and the team at Wiley for backing me for a second book
- Dana Rousmaniere for giving me a shot at writing several articles for *Harvard Business Review* that have morphed and evolved into this book
- everybody who picked up a copy of *Employee to Entrepreneur* — especially those of you who took some time to personally write me or share your positive sentiments online
- media representatives the world over who have time and time again given me exposure in their publications.

Mostly, thanks goes out to you, for picking up a copy of this book.

What would make me an order of magnitude more grateful is if you went a step further and began to apply the concepts within this book, made a fundamental positive change in your life, and shared this online with your network, or even wrote me personally.

It's doing work that matters that leaves me feeling fulfilled, and knowing that my work is making a difference is everything.

Preface

I had just emerged from another three-hour meeting, where 11 of my colleagues and I were briefed on an upcoming client engagement.

In truth, 10 of us were there to contribute for all of five minutes, while two people led the monologue.

When I looked around the room, most people were preoccupied with their smartphones, their email or staring into space, perhaps contemplating what they'd have for dinner that night, not to mention opportunity cost.

The ding of desktop and smartphone notifications was unrelenting, and it was clear that most people were only physically present.

Nonetheless, these were three hours that they, nor the organisation that was paying them each a six-figure salary to be there, wouldn't get back. From the organisation's perspective, this was a 36-hour meeting, and given the seniority around the table, it set the company back about five thousand dollars in payroll and on-costs.

Having attended several of these routine meetings in the previous few weeks, and found each one as equally useless as the last, I challenged my manager.

'Isn't there a better way to prepare for these gigs than a three-hour meeting every time?'

'It's a necessary evil,' I was told.

I soon left the organisation to pursue entrepreneurship.

It became apparent to me over the next few years that it wasn't a necessary evil. It was just a form of consensus-seeking, symptomatic of an organisation devoid of trust between its people, and a culture that was not inclined to experiment with alternative, and potentially better, ways of working.

Nowadays, I'm blessed to head up an organisation that is the antithesis of the abovementioned. We only have meetings if they're absolutely necessary, and set default meeting times to 15 minutes. If somebody doesn't need to be there or can relay whatever information they have to share via email or instant message, that's what they do. We can't steal time in our colleagues' calendars without their permission and without a legitimate reason for meeting.

Since 2015, we've gone from upstart to one of Australia's fastest growing new companies, having worked with over 50 huge brands around the world and incubated over 100 startups as part of our corporate-startup partnership programs.

Not only that, but we've also established Lemonade Stand, our children's entrepreneurship program, that now exists as a workshop and an online SaaS platform.

We spun off Konkrete, a blockchain-enabled share registry we founded.

I wrote several books, including two for Wiley—one of which you hold in your hands right now — and a children's picture book!

And I found time to host the *Future Squared* podcast, which, as of writing, is over 370 episodes strong.

It's painfully clear to me, having spent a decade in the corporate world, and now consulting to many large corporations, that my team and I are untold times more productive than the typical company, on a per capita basis.

But startups aren't exempt too. Having worked with hundreds of entrepreneurs, they too have a tendency to adopt the same practices that run riot in the corporate world, and fall victim to all sorts of biological tendencies to do the easiest thing first—the thing that makes us feel busy and important, but doesn't actually move the needle forward at all.

In December 2018, I reflected on how we go about creating value, and captured my findings in a short piece for *Harvard Business Review* called 'The Case for the 6-Hour Workday'.

Within weeks of the article going live, it not only received thousands of engagements online, but it was syndicated by media outlets across the globe such as *The Wall Street Journal, CNBC, Fast Company,* News.com.au, *The New Zealand Herald, Yahoo! News, Tech in Asia, La Información, Smart Company, Indian Management* and *European CEO,* and translated into several languages, including Russian, Korean, Spanish and Persian.

This interest suggested that our way of work was still a distant dream for most organisations.

Millions of people still work long hours, attend pointless meetings, and spend their workdays glued to their inbox, playing a digital game of Whack-a-Mole, but come the end of the day they have nothing to show for it.

Contrary to what some might have you believe, these dated hallmarks of the corporate world aren't a necessary evil; they're stupid and counterproductive.

But it doesn't have to be this way.

Adopting a better way of work doesn't have to be a distant dream.

Having spent years as both an entrepreneur and corporate executive, I know that large organisations, SMEs and startups alike can use the tools and techniques I put forward in this book to radically improve their own effectiveness. Heck, anybody creating anything of value and wanting to earn themselves more time, either to re-invest into business interests or into life, can reap significant measurable benefits through the tools and techniques presented.

As we'll learn, it's not just about making people more productive in the office, but about freeing up precious hours for living life, which, paradoxically, has a positive effect on performance in the office.

That's why I wrote this book.

It picks up where my *HBR* article left off, and provides you, the reader, with an actionable playbook for increasing your productivity and enjoyment of life, many times over.

When my 68-year-old mum, who still speaks with a strong Eastern European accent, asked me what this book was about, I explained it as follows.

Business is really hard. It can be like rolling a big boulder uphill. You have to invest a lot of energy to get to the top of the hill.

But once you're there, you can roll it downhill, and it doesn't take anywhere near as much effort.

But so many people keep exerting themselves as if they're still pushing uphill when they're at the summit.

They continue to work 12-hour days, despite new technologies that can make their lives easier. They continue to work 12-hour days but most of them would get the same results with six.

This book, I told her, is about helping people sit down to watch the boulder roll down to the bottom, sip some water (or wine!) and take in the sunset.

It can just as well help those still rolling the boulder uphill to get to the summit.

Introduction

When you hear the word 'rich', what pops into your mind? Chauffered cars, beach houses, yachts and 18-hole country clubs perhaps?

Here's the thing.

You probably have access to all of these things.

Sharing economy platforms such as Airbnb give us access to resources once exclusively the domain of the wealthy.

Access is usually better than ownership because it comes without the cost and headache overhead.

As the old adage goes, the happiest days in a boat owner's life are the days they bought and sold their boat.

Despite inflation effectively devaluing a currency over time, one dollar today buys us exponentially more than it ever has before across myriad areas. As *The Washington Times* pointed out in an article, 'Common folk live better now than royalty did in earlier times'.

The average American on US$25 000 per year lives in a home with air conditioning, refrigeration, a shower with running warm water, a washing machine, a television and the internet—and probably eats a lot more calories than they should.

Louis XIV, the French king who ruled from 1643 to 1715, lived in constant fear of dying from smallpox. So too did John D Rockefeller, the richest man in the world 100 years ago. When was the last time you heard of anybody dying from the plague?

Count your blessings that we live in a time of antibiotics and vaccines. Critical healthcare has become almost ubiquitous over the past century, with 84 per cent of kids around the world having received three doses of the tetanus shot.

We have more access to information and education than we know what to meaningfully do with. That supercomputer you carry in your pocket would have cost tens of millions of dollars in the 1960s (if it had existed back then).

There is so much social narrative that demonises the '1 per cent', but if you make more than US$32400, you are in the global 1 per cent.

Want to travel to the other side of the world tomorrow? There's no doubt an airline will get you there, well within your budget, with the price of airline travel falling 50 per cent in the past 40 years.

And let's not forget all of the creature comforts of modern life: think avocado smash, almond milk lattes and kombucha tea!

Angus Deaton and Daniel Kahneman's oft-cited Nobel Prize-winning study on the link between money and happiness found that, beyond US$75000, money doesn't make us measurably happier.

In short—we are all richer than ever before.

But we are poorer than ever before as well ... poorer than ever when it comes to our time.

The average person:

- works 40 to 44 hours a week
- spends five hours commuting per week
- spends 10 to 15 hours running errands per week.

That's a total of about 60 hours a week.

Factor in the eight hours of sleep a night you should be getting and you're left with 50 hours a week.

This is to say nothing of people who routinely work 60 to 80 hours per week.

And how do we choose to spend that time?

Staring at screens.

The average person spends 11 hours a day staring at screens: this translates to two-thirds of their waking hours.

What use is being rich if you spend 70 per cent of your time staring at screens, and the rest running errands or sitting in mind-numbing meetings where nothing gets achieved?

That doesn't sound like a rich life, no matter how many zeros you have in your bank account.

What use is having access to a boat if you never have the time to take it out?

What use is all of that money in the bank if you never have time to spend it?

As Roman philosopher Seneca put it in his essay *On The Shortness of Life,*

> people are frugal in guarding their personal property; but as soon as it comes to squandering time they are most wasteful of the one thing in which it is right to be stingy ... It is not that we have so little time but that we lose so much. ... The life we receive is not short but we make it so; we are not ill provided but use what we have wastefully.

We think nothing of giving people our time—something we can never get back once used—saying 'yes' to all sorts of nonsensical requests for our time, but when it comes to our money, we will skimp wherever we can, with some people walking an extra five minutes to save $2 on ATM transaction fees. But money, unlike time, can be earned back.

In a world of resource abundance but time scarcity, what it means to be rich is changing.

As Warren Buffett famously said, 'the rich invest in time, the poor invest in money'.

Investing in time gives us deeper personal relationships, more time in nature and more well-adjusted physical and emotional health; it empowers us to contribute to our communities, to travel (not just for business) and to take up new hobbies ... and it also helps us kick arse in the office.

Time—not just our salaries or financial investments—is what gives us a rich life.

There are countless books on becoming financially rich, but how do we become time rich?

It's not enough just to think differently.

It's time to work differently and live differently.

PART 1
HOW WE GOT HERE

American poet Maya Angelou once said that 'if you don't know where you've come from, you don't know where you're going.'

In order to better navigate the world around us, we must understand the origin story and the mechanics of the system we find ourselves in. Only then can we fully appreciate its shortcomings and readjust to change course.

CHAPTER 1
Origins of the eight-hour workday

Mass production, the spinning jenny and the steam engine. These are hallmarks of the Industrial Revolution, a time when humankind arguably took great strides forward.

This era has been broken into two stages by historians. The first stage, from 1770 to 1870, brought about a shift away from agriculture thanks to steam, iron and water. The second stage spanned from 1870 through to World War I in 1914, which featured the advent of electricity, the internal combustion engine, oil and steel.

Life expectancy among children increased dramatically, with the under-five mortality rate in London decreasing from 745 in 1730 to 318 in 1810.

Street lighting, drinkable water, drainage and sewage disposal became commonplace in developed economies, leading to better sanitation, general health of the populace and a downturn in disease.

The increase in population density in urban areas, as well as the economic shifts of the time, paved the way for an increase in schools and literacy, mostly because the biggest hurdle to education had been overcome — proximity.

Numerous other game-changing innovations emerged from the Industrial Revolution. Among them are:

- James Watt developed the steam engine in the 1760s, which paved the way for rapid advancements in factory output as well as both commercial and passenger transportation.
- Edmund Cartwright gave us the power loom in 1787, enabling mass production of cloth.
- Richard Trevithick invented the steam train in 1806, followed by George Stephenson's *Rocket* in 1829.
- Abraham Darby developed smelting iron, enabling higher production of iron for buildings and the railways that Stephenson's *Rocket* would travel on.
- Thomas Telford and John McAdam developed tarmacked roads, with strong foundations, a smooth surface and proper drainage.
- Michael Faraday, Thomas Edison and Nikola Tesla's work combined to give us the electricity we know today, convertible to heat, light and motion.
- Alexander Graham Bell gave us the telephone in 1876, and Guglielmo Marconi the radio in 1895.

During this time of transformation, middle, upper and aristocratic classes rode the wave of improved economic and living standards. Astonishingly, while it took four days to travel from London to Manchester in 1700, by 1870 the trip had been reduced to just four hours. This isn't much longer than the two-hour trip passengers can expect aboard a National Rail train today.

Humanity obtained a vastly more significant understanding of the world, thanks to the many industrial and scientific discoveries of the time.

All of this progress came at a cost to the environment (including the depletion of natural resources, increased air and water pollution, and an increase in fossil fuel consumption), to the working class and to the poor.

The latter had to contend with grim, hazardous and monotonous working conditions, and miserable, disease-prone living conditions.

From the cradle to the coal mine

Working-class children weren't spared either. Children as young as four worked long and dangerous hours in production factories and coal mines where they would crawl through tunnels that were too small for adults. There, they would drag carts weighing 70 kilograms by a chain attached to their waist for distances of up to 50 metres (see figure 1.1).

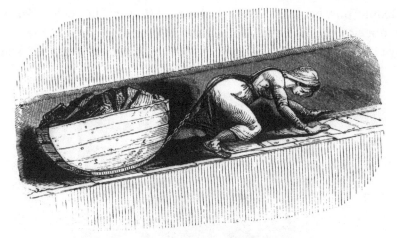

Figure 1.1: a child dragging a coal cart in a tunnel
Source: The Print Collector / Alamy Stock Photo

The British Royal Commission of Inquiry into Children's Employment (1842) presented the following interviews to Parliament, painting a vivid picture of the horrific conditions.

> I have been driving horses since I was seven but for one year before that I looked after an air door. I would like to go to school but I am too tired as I work for twelve hours.
> **Philip Davies, aged 10, Dinas Colliery, Rhondda**

> We are doorkeepers in the four-foot level. We leave the house before six each morning and are in the level until seven o'clock and sometimes later. We get 2p a day and our light costs us 2½p a week. Rachel was in a day school and she can read a little. She was run over by a dram a while ago and was home ill a long time, but she has got over it.
> **Elizabeth Williams, aged 10 and Mary and Rachel Enoch, 11 and 12 respectively, Dowlais Pits, Merthyr**

When I got my fingers fast it was awful. I went through so much pain and I was only a little girl and, of course I couldn't work. I lost four fingers in all ... that was the end of my career in cotton.

Oldham cotton mill worker

Most children weren't insured until the age of 16, so if they were injured and couldn't work, they either had to find another job or fight for compensation, which they couldn't afford to do.

Iconic photographs taken by Lewis Hine, a US sociologist and member of the National Child Labor Committee during the 1910s powerfully captured the plight of working children in the US south (see figure 1.2).

Figure 1.2: a young boy working as a coal miner, c. 1910
Source: Lewis Hine

It's estimated that one-fifth of Britain's textile industry workers were under the age of 15 in the 1860s, while two-thirds of the cotton mill workers were children.

Similarly, in the United States an estimated 1.7 million children were employed in industrial roles at the dawn of the 20th century.

Karl Marx believed that capitalism was inherently unfair and was an outspoken critic of child labour. The socialist philosopher and revolutionary famously said that US capital was financed by the 'capitalized blood of children'.

The monotony of work

Textiles was the dominant industry of the Industrial Revolution. Workers toiled away in dirty factories to produce varieties of cotton, wool and silk. The spinning jenny, invented by James Hargreaves in 1764, helped textile workers to produce yarn, and was to textiles what the printing press was to books.

If it wasn't a textiles factory, then it was a coal mine, a steel mill, a glass, cement or chemical factory, or laying the foundations for our roads and railroads.

The Second Agricultural Revolution dovetailed with the Industrial Revolution. It was characterised by new techniques such as crop rotation, selective breeding, better transport, and, of course, economies of scale from larger farms. For the purposes of this book, we will consider these two revolutions synonymously as they each represented a technological upheaval and mass production and they occurred simultaneously.

The shift in agricultural practices meant more production from fewer farmers, leading to a surplus of workers. Now free to work in factories, this made the industrial job market incredibly competitive.

Despite being in high demand, industrial jobs were repetitive, algorithmic and monotonous.

Mechanisation and mass production may have been economically attractive, but they had less than desirable effects on the workers.

Rather than revel in the accomplishment-driven dopamine high that comes with seeing a product through to the end, machines subdivided production into small, repetitive tasks with individual workers performing only a single task. This was in stark contrast to the craftsmanship of earlier times.

Measuring productivity

Several factors are used to measure manufacturing productivity. Of these, total factor productivity (TFP)—or multifactor productivity (MFP)—has for a long time been the widely accepted norm.

TFP compares the number of goods and services produced (output) to the number of combined inputs used to produce those goods and services. Figure 1.3 depicts an example of this.

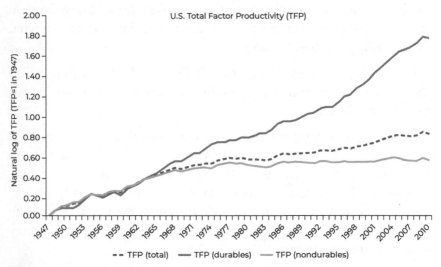

Figure 1.3: US total factor productivity, 1947
Source: US Bureau of Statistics

What mattered most during the Industrial Revolution was the number of widgets built, sold and delivered over a given period of time; namely, sheer output.

The easiest way to amplify output and satisfy economic interests? Amplify inputs. In the case of the Industrial Revolution, aside from technology optimisation, this meant cranking up inputs such as hours worked and cadence of work.

As such, the workday was not only monotonous, but it was long, and the pace of work was painfully fast.

Worker exploitation

Adults and children alike were paid a pittance in wages, with children earning just 10 to 20 per cent of what the already poorly remunerated adults were.

After several decades of the Industrial Revolution, urban areas had become crowded, and this, together with improved TFP, meant that supply exceeded demand. As a result, a long line of desperate people were willing to do any kind of work so long as they got paid.

Captains of industry took advantage of this fact, cranking up hours while paying workers just enough so that they were struggling to survive, perpetuating a dire existence: 10 shillings per week for men, 5 shillings for women and 1 shilling for children (1 shilling is equivalent to US$8 today).

Twelve- to 16-hour days and six-day weeks were the norm for most industrial workers of the time, with a one-hour break per day and no paid leave. Taking leave meant vacating your post, which in an incredibly competitive job market was not an option.

Occupational health and safety standards didn't exist and accidents inevitably happened regularly. Workers were unfamiliar with the machines; they had to crawl under them, and many children were killed or crushed under the force of these machines. In 1833, Britain's Factory Act was introduced to improve conditions for children in factories, and in 1844, fencing machinery was made compulsory.

A memo from the Quarry Bank Mill in Cheshire, England, reads as follows:

On 23rd June 1845, an accident resulting fatally happened to a weaving over looker's assistant named Joseph Davenport, some 25 years of age. While engaged in doing some job about a loom, the buckle of a strap caught his shirt sleeve and snatched him up to the drum, and wrenched his arm off at the shoulder. He was immediately removed to the Manchester Infirmary where he died after lingering for a few days.

The temperature in textile spinning rooms would reach 70 degrees Fahrenheit (21 degrees Celsius), and floors were slippery, being covered in water and oil. Sanitary conditions in the mills left a lot to be desired, with both sexes often sharing one toilet, usually situated in view of workers. Workers would complain of the smell emanating from the toilets.

Timber, naked lights, flammable cotton and the friction from continuously moving machinery all combined to render the cotton mills fire and death traps. In New Lanark, Scotland, three out of its four mills were burned to the ground.

The poor living and working conditions were a significant factor in average life expectancy, which in 1837, was in the high 30s (unadjusted for child mortality) and it was lower for factory workers.

'8 hours labour, 8 hours recreation, 8 hours rest'

In 1817, Welsh textile manufacturer and social reformer Robert Owen formulated the goal of the eight-hour workday, coining the slogan '8 hours labour, 8 hours recreation, 8 hours rest'. This sparked the '8-hour day movement' or what was then known as the 'short-time movement'.

Karl Marx saw the eight-hour day as vital to workers' health. He wrote in *Das Kapital* in 1867 that, 'by extending the working day, therefore, capitalist production...not only produces a deterioration of human labour-power by robbing it of its normal moral and physical conditions of development and activity, but also produces the premature exhaustion and death of this labour power itself.'

Regardless of your political or economic dispositions, Marx did have a point.

An eight-hour day became the chief demand of labour unions in the 1870s, followed by the establishment of a network of Eight-Hour Leagues, which held protests across the United States.

Labour unions and the eight-hour workday

Labour unions, formed to protect the interests of workers, had for a long time been outlawed in Britain as a result of the Combination Act of 1799, which criminalised unionising and protesting for better working conditions. Unions were eventually legalised as part of the Royal Commission of 1867, around the same time that US unions emerged.

The first US unions were small and native to town or state.

National unions began to form after the American Civil War. The unions actively fought for better wages, reasonable hours and safer working conditions through strikes and diligent political manoeuvring.

In 1914, the Ford Motor Company radically doubled wages and cut shift hours from nine to eight, increasing Ford's productivity and profit margin (margins doubled from $30 million to $60 million in just two years—a feat most of today's private equity firms would be proud of).

Inspired by Ford's heroics, other companies quickly followed suit, and countries did too. It was around this time that Uruguay became the first country to adopt the eight-hour working day nationwide.

Slowly but surely, the chips began to fall as different industries and geographies earned their eight-hour day.

The eight-hour day was finally ratified in 1938 by the Fair Labor Standards Act. This made the eight-hour day a reality for most working Americans.

Old habits die hard

It seems that we've yet to learn anything from Ford's 1914 experiment and the doubling of margins that cutting hours and increasing wages had on its workforce.

Nor have we learned anything from the experiences of craftsmen and women of the Industrial Revolution, whose craft was reduced to the demoralising drudgery of being just another cog in a machine. Only the extrinsic reward of a pay cheque and their innate desire for survival motivated them to keep showing up at work.

Today, the nature of work is increasingly becoming much more like that of pre-industrialised crafts: it requires focus, critical thinking and creativity. However, most large organisations still treat their people like automatons, conflating output with hours worked.

Unfortunately, the net result isn't one of economic boom.

Most white-collar organisations have a culture steeped in the dated management practices of the factory floor, with one of the most significant hallmarks of this being the eight-hour workday. We'll explore this disconnect between the nature of work and management practices in the next chapter.

CHAPTER 2
The evolution of work

So much has changed since the eight-hour workday was ratified into law in the United States in 1938.

The internet fundamentally changed the way we live, work and play. The nature of work has transitioned in large part from algorithmic tasks to heuristic ones that require critical thinking, problem solving and creativity.

From the farm to the factory

In 1840, 69 per cent of the US labour force was employed in agriculture. As a result of growing efficiencies in farming practices, this number had fallen to 38 per cent by 1900, and today just 1.6 per cent of Americans work in agriculture — that's a 43-fold decrease.

Manufacturing and commodities industries too have suffered a similar fate.

According to the US Bureau of Labor Statistics, more than 30 per cent of the non-farm US labour force was employed in manufacturing in 1940; today, less than 10 per cent is.

In fact, manufacturing, construction and mining *combined* command just 12.6 per cent of its labour force.

Figure 2.1 (overleaf) illustrates manufacturing employment as a percentage of non-farm employment over this period of time.

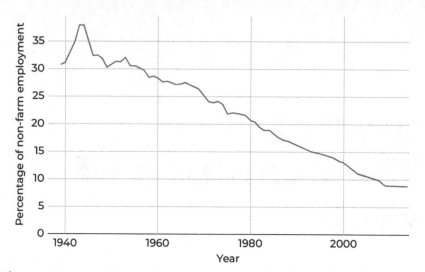

Figure 2.1: manufacturing employment in the United States, from 1940 to now
Source: Bureau of Labor Statistics

The rise of critical thinking

The labour force changed in other ways as well during the 20th century.

It has in large part transitioned away from carrying out process-oriented tasks, and moved towards engaging in critical-thinking tasks: tasks that require navigating complex problems and people.

The overwhelming majority of Americans today are employed in the services industry (80.3 per cent).

This includes professional and business services (12.9 per cent), healthcare (13.8 per cent), hospitality (10.1 per cent), state and local government (12.1 per cent), retail trade (9.7 per cent) and financial activities (5.2 per cent).

In 1950, only 33 per cent of US women of working age were employed; by 1998, 60 per cent were employed. Among women aged 25 to 34, the participation rate more than doubled from 34 per cent in 1950 to 76.3 per cent in 1998.

In Australia, only half of working-age females were employed in 1978; 40 years later, this number stood at 73.3 per cent.

Rise of the machines

Machines have replaced workers across numerous industries and tasks during the past three centuries, and especially over the past 70 years.

According to a report by the Oxford Martin School, over the long term, technology has always created more jobs than it has destroyed.

Today, most economic discussions about automation and artificial intelligence inevitably end up exploring the merits of universal basic income (UBI), as fears of robot-induced unemployment dominate the conversation.

The US National Research Council found that work shifted across four significant dimensions in the 20th century:

1. *autonomy-control:* the degree of discretion and decision-making power workers have
2. *task scope:* the breadth of tasks embedded into a job
3. *cognitive complexity:* the degree of cognitive activity and analysis required
4. *interactive dimensions:* the extent to which the quality of social interactions, including their emotional quality, is critical to job performance.

The latter includes emotional labour, which in the 20 years since the National Research Council identified these shifts, has become known as emotional intelligence (EQ).

Many pundits today are suggesting that EQ is more important than IQ when it comes to succeeding in the modern world.

This changing nature of work has meant that you might find yourself doing something that didn't exist 30 years ago, let alone during the Industrial Revolution. Here's a snapshot of *some* jobs that didn't exist 30 years ago:

- blogger
- data scientist
- social media manager
- digital marketer

- genetic counsellor
- podcaster
- solar photovoltaic installer
- cloud architect
- app developer
- information security analyst
- user experience designer
- drone operator ...

I had to stop myself there. The list is long. And it's set to get even longer.

According to the World Economic Forum, 65 per cent of children entering primary school today will end up working in jobs that aren't on our radar yet. A 15 year old today is expected to have 17 jobs and five different careers over their lifetime.

The Institute for the Future (IFTF) echoes this thinking, suggesting that 85 per cent of the jobs that will exist in 2030 haven't even been invented yet.

This is because we find ourselves in the midst of what is being dubbed the Fourth Industrial Revolution. Advanced robotics, autonomous transport, artificial intelligence, advanced materials, biotechnology and genomics, among other things, are all combining to re-shape the way we live and work.

Today's digital economy has delivered a fundamental shift in the nature of our organisations. Physical presence is no longer a prerequisite to doing business. Automattic, the company behind the WordPress platform that powers 30 per cent of the internet, has 700 employees spread across 62 countries. Instead of offices, the company provides workers with a US$250-a-month stipend to spend at co-working spaces (or in a Starbucks).

Companies deliver online services from remote parts of the globe, and profit from software and intellectual property. Organisations in the digital economy can evolve much faster from startup to behemoth, often with few employees or tangible assets. In 2012, photography behemoth Kodak, which employed thousands, filed for bankruptcy. That same year, photo-sharing platform Instagram, which boasts having just 13 employees, was sold to Facebook for US$1 billion.

Automation is taking greater hold over not just blue-collar, but also white-collar jobs, which to this day are given the 'safe and secure' stamp of approval by unsuspecting and ill-informed parents and career counsellors the world over.

According to US non-profit membership media organisation NPR, accountants and auditors face a 93.5 per cent chance of being automated; legal secretaries a 97.6 per cent chance; and real estate agents an 86.4 per cent chance.

Deloitte too gives the jobs of appraisers and assessors of real estate a 90 per cent chance of being performed by bots.

This all points to a society that increasingly values thought over mindlessly following procedure. To compete in a fast-changing job economy, you will need to do more of the former, and less of the latter.

This changing nature of organisations and work has resulted in a shift in demand for skills among workers. The demand for process-oriented skills that can be automated is declining in line with the declining cost of automation tools.

Deloitte estimates that the cost of a single bot—the software that could automate part of a process—fell more than 95 per cent from $500 000 in 2008 to $22 000 in 2018.

The cost, in many ways, is actually much lower. Startups and SMEs are tapping into the power of automation tools across their entire value chains. Many such tools only cost them between US$10 and US$100 a month.

I once paid my then 15-year-old nephew, Nicholas, $10 an hour to identify potential prospects via LinkedIn and send them personalised messages. Nowadays, I use a tool to automate this for me at 10 times the speed, and at 5 per cent the cost. Sorry Nicholas—a valuable lesson in adaptability learned young (at least that's my story and I'm sticking to it!).

Conversely, the demand for advanced cognitive skills, socio-behavioural skills and greater adaptability are all rising.

The future of jobs

The World Economic Forum's Future of Jobs Report 2018 listed the following 10 skills as critical to surviving and thriving in 2020:

1. complex problem solving
2. critical thinking
3. creativity
4. management
5. coordinating with others
6. emotional intelligence
7. judgement and decision making
8. service orientation
9. negotiation
10. cognitive flexibility.

This ties in with a report from the US General Services Administration which found that the nature of work today is more cognitively complex, collaborative, dependent on social skills and technological competence, time pressured, mobile and competitive.

This shows up in white-collar and blue-collar jobs because the Industrial Revolution-inspired division of labour that supported mass production isn't compatible with current markets.

As we've explored, mass production emphasised quantity over quality, and repetitive specialised tasks that required low discretion and skill. However, today's markets increasingly demand quality, innovation and customisation, while repetitive specialised tasks are increasingly being automated.

Amazon's director of robotics and fulfillment, Scott Andersen, says that Amazon's warehouses will be fully, end-to-end automated in about ten years—not that long in the greater scheme of things.

This is why Alec Ross, Barack Obama's former technology adviser and author of *The Industries of the Future*, says that there will be no room for mediocrity when it comes to the future of work. You won't be able to simply coast by: organisations will be looking to optimise for performance in a way that they have never had to before.

This is being demonstrated today by the growing gap between labour productivity and compensation. Having increased in lockstep with labour productivity throughout the 20th century, nonsupervisory compensation stalled around 1980, as can be seen in figure 2.2. This reflected both automation and less value being placed on such roles by society, something Ross warned us of.

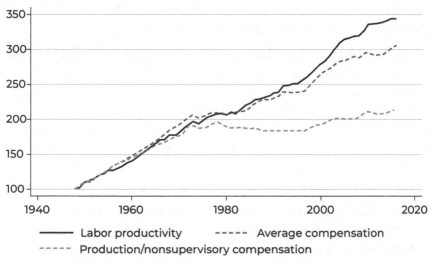

Figure 2.2: labour productivity versus average compensation
Source: US Bureau of Statistics

Given the competitiveness of the digital economy, the organisations that succeed are more likely to be lean and agile, less hierarchical, less likely to provide lifelong job security and continually reorganising to adapt to external changes.

'How big is your company?'

Human beings are social animals. Like a peacock signalling reproductive fitness with its large and colourful tail, human beings signal through our haircuts, clothes, the cars we drive, the places we live, what we eat, what we *don't* eat, when we wake up, how often we work out, the titles on our business cards... the list goes on.

If you're an entrepreneur or executive, you might have signalled your worth by sharing with others just how many people you have working for you. At the very least, you've no doubt been asked the status intelligence-gathering question, 'How big is your team?' before.

Once upon a time, the size of your team was indeed a reflection of the value of your company. And here's why.

The late Nobel Prize winner and British economist Ronald Coase put forward a timeless theory back in 1937. In an article dubbed 'The Nature of the Firm', Coase offered an economic explanation as to why companies emerge. He found that companies tend to hire employees rather than trade on the open market because, as deliverables become more complex, external transaction costs exceed internal transaction costs — essentially, that it's cheaper to do the work in-house than hire contractors.

Coase noted that the cost of obtaining a good or service externally is actually more than just the price of the good. Costs extend to search, reconnaissance, bargaining, intellectual property protection, on-boarding, training, monitoring and compliance costs.

Firms emerge because they arrange themselves to produce what they need internally so that they can mitigate or avoid these costs.

Coase argued that arms-length transactions (like buying a coffee) and basic contractual arrangements could be performed externally more cheaply than they could internally (see figure 2.3). However, it makes less sense to do more complex contracts and transactions externally. Vertical integration refers to complex transactions whereby there is a need for synchronous communication and integration with upstream and downstream activities.

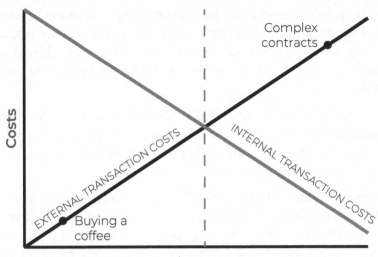

Figure 2.3: the nature of firms

Coase observed that firms grew — in terms of headcount — so long as the grey line stayed below the black line in figure 2.3. Firms would take the more complex transactions in-house, and therefore stimulate their growth by way of headcount.

The World Bank found, in its report 'The Changing Nature of Work', that the internet, free trade agreements and improved infrastructure have reduced the cost of external transactions, including cross-border trade, allowing for transactions to take place wherever costs are lower. The report found that 'new technologies have lowered communication costs. As a result, firms are less vertically integrated, and managers are outsourcing more tasks to the market'.

It cites JD.com, China's second-largest e-commerce company, as an example of this. The company has more than 170 000 online merchants on its platform, many in rural areas.

Headcount, to those in the know, is losing its veneer as a signalling mechanism because it is no longer directly correlated with the value of an organisation. The badge of honour for an entrepreneur or leader today may be creating as much value with as little internal headcount as possible, with a globally distributed team of contractors and sophisticated algorithms working in lockstep with one another.

On the flipside, as organisations become bigger and more bloated by way of headcount, internal transaction costs grow. Communication becomes a nightmare and accountability is spread thin due to multiple-hour meetings with far too many people sitting around the table.

Eventually, internal costs reach that of external costs. This is when external markets beat firms. At this point, firms are merely trying to survive rather than innovate, something former industry giants such as Blockbuster know all too well.

Despite having—at the time of writing—only 7000 employees, Netflix has a market capitalisation of over US$136 billion. Compare this with Blockbuster, which at its peak had over 60 000 employees but was worth just US$5 billion. Amazon makes twice as much revenue per employee as its bricks-and-mortar rival, Walmart, but employs less than one-third the number of people: it effectively makes six times more per person.

What kind of organisation would you rather be? A fat, bloated one with a slim revenue-per-employee ratio, or a small organisation that punches orders of magnitude above its literal and proverbial weight?

Business model for the new economy

In light of these changes, Tim O'Reilly of O'Reilly Media, and author of *WTF: What's the Future and Why It's Up to Us*, coined the business model map for the next economy.

O'Reilly's model showed that in order for companies to be competitive in the digital economy, they should ensure their business model aligns with that of the new economy, characterised by on-demand talent and services, automation and a magical user experience.

On-demand talent and resources has come to embody some of the venture-backed tech success stories of the day such as Uber, Airbnb and Upwork. The gig economy was estimated to be worth US$3.7 trillion by SIA as at October 2018, and this number continues to grow.

Today 56.7 million Americans are doing freelance work, up by 3.7 million since 2014, and these jobs extend to computer programming, penetration testing, social media marketing, tutoring, home maintenance, delivery, driving for a ride-sharing company, providing care, sales and odd jobs.

These jobs give people the freedom and flexibility that they may struggle to find in traditional permanent employment. Freedom to choose what to do, and where and when to do it. Flexibility to manage a schedule in accordance with a chosen lifestyle.

For most of these jobs, algorithm-driven platforms augment job prospects, but also client–vendor relationships. This is true of Upwork, the global freelancing marketplace that was valued at US$1.55 billion at the time of writing.

The internet makes it possible for today's organisations, such as the 'Airbnb for X' marketplaces, to do what only exceedingly large organisations could do previously. Nowadays, you can use Squarespace to build your company website, Stripe to accept payments, Facebook to run some ads, and Google Analytics to measure the results — all in a weekend, and all for less than $100. Doing the same 20 years ago would have set you back tens, if not hundreds, of thousands, of dollars.

Awareness of this new business model and way of working is step 1 towards playing 21st century ball.

Exponential technology

The rate at which companies on the S&P 500 Index are being replaced is increasing, with the average lifespan of a company on the index falling from 61 years in 1958 to just 18 years today.

While 20th century management theories might have worked at a time when the rate of change was slow, many of them are redundant today. Yet the majority of organisations still rely on them.

Throughout the 1990s, Moore's Law—the doubling of computing power every 18 to 24 months—took the transistor count per microchip from 1 million to more than 100 million—a 100-times increase.

However, from 2010 to 2016 alone, we added more than 10 billion transistors—a 10 000-times increase.

And the rate is accelerating.

This exponential growth in technology (illustrated in figure 2.4) has brought us to an inflection point, and it is presenting today's business executives with more change and uncertainty than ever before.

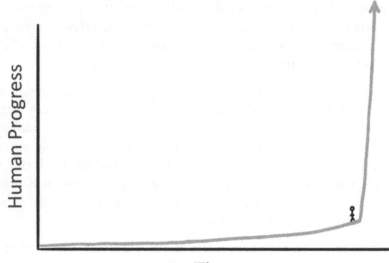

waitbutwhy.com

Figure 2.4: human progress over time
Source: Tim Urban, Waitbutwhy.com

While one would, today, no doubt need degrees of interpersonal skills and problem solving on the factory floor, particularly in a supervisory role, the overarching skillset required to thrive in a production role during the early 20th century would have boiled down to the following:

- follow procedure
- act quickly
- maintain attention to detail
- effectively communicate issues.

In short, show up and do as you're told.

All work wasn't created equal

When it comes to heuristic work, increasing not just the quantity but also the quality of output isn't a matter of working longer hours or trying to work faster. The opposite is true.

Research suggests that the average worker is only productive for two hours and 53 minutes in an eight-hour workday.

Adam Grant, leading organisational psychologist and *New York Times* bestselling author of *Originals: How Non-Conformists Move the World*, says that 'the more complex and creative jobs are, the less it makes sense to pay attention to hours at all'.

Yet despite all of this, the eight-hour workday, testament to 19th century socialist movements and more suited to algorithmic jobs, still prevails.

'Like most humans,' Grant says, 'leaders are remarkably good at anchoring on the past even when it's irrelevant to the present.'

CALL TO ACTION

Reflect on your job.

1. How does your job relate to the National Research Council's four dimensions of work?

2. Did your job exist 30 years ago?

3. Is your job subject to automation in the near future? (Check out bit.ly/nprbot.)

4. Which of the World Economic Forum's 10 key skills do you not possess or need to develop further?

5. Is your organisation built around a world where external transaction costs are lower than internal costs, or is it still operating as if little has changed outside its walls?

6. Which of Tim O'Reilly's elements feature (or could feature) in your organisation's business model?

PART 2
THE PSYCHOLOGY OF WORK

Since we were young kids in school, we have only ever learned *what* to do.

The same holds true in the workplace. But nobody ever shone a spotlight on *how* to work. If our ability to think is what distinguishes us from the rest of the animal kingdom, why has learning how to best work not formed part of school curriculums or workplace learning and development programs?

CHAPTER 3
The flow state

'Why are you always working so late?' I asked a colleague from a big four firm. They told me that they usually work until 10 pm, and sometimes even into the morning hours.

The response was a predictable one: 'I can't leave until my boss does.'

'Are you actually getting much done in the evening?' I asked.

'Not really.'

This plays out all too often at large professional services firms (and profit-seeking enterprises in general) where hours worked is wrongfully conflated with productivity.

And I get it. Hours are far easier to categorise and make sense of than output, which is a lot more arbitrary in a heuristic working world.

The reality is that after you've worked a certain number of hours, the connection between effort and reward is no longer linear. The diminishing law of returns takes hold.

What we should be managing instead of time is attention. Attention is becoming increasingly hijacked in a world of 'attention merchants' luring us away with real-time notifications.

You've probably found yourself deeply immersed in an activity when the rest of the world ceased to be. You checked the time, and you were surprised to see that hours had gone by. You were in what psychologists call 'the flow state'.

First coined by Hungarian-American psychologist Mihaly Csikszentmihalyi in 1975, you might also know 'flow' as 'the zone' or 'deep work'.

But it's more than that.

At its core, flow is *living*, rather than merely existing.

LET'S CATCH SOME BRAIN WAVES, BRAH!

Of the five brain waves, theta, alpha and gamma show up during flow.

Theta is a highly creative zone that invites vivid visualisations and profound insights. This is where the potential for spiritual experiences and a sense of connectedness, otherwise reached through deep meditation, occurs.

Alpha is a meditative state in which memory, learning and concentration are heightened. Our awareness of our surroundings expands, and we mostly have a higher degree of presence in the moment.

Gamma waves are responsible for bursts of insight and high-level information processing, combining disparate ideas into a single idea—the essence of creativity.

Flow occurs at the intersection of the alpha and theta brain waves, with gamma waves making a cameo.

It's at the intersection of awareness, creativity and insights that we become our best.

Interestingly, you can monitor brain waves using devices such as the Muse headband. Not only that, but if you want to geek out and get super precise when it comes to measuring your, and your team's, performance, you can use such devices to determine:

» what kind of work triggers the flow state, and what inhibits it

» in what kind of environment and at what time of day people get into flow

» how much time people spend in flow.

With this information, you can create an environment where you and your team spend as much time in flow as possible.

Picture a lone surfer paddling furiously as they match the speed of an incoming two-metre wave, pop up onto their feet and ride the ensuing barrel. At that moment, a surfer isn't thinking about the bills they need to pay or the arguments they may have had with their partner earlier that day. If they are, then they're unlikely to catch the wave.

When a surfer catches a wave, they're in total flow — deeply immersed in the act of surfing — and in their mind, the rest of the world simply ceases to exist.

The flow state extends beyond just the athletic domains. It extends to our work. It's critical to heuristic work such as writing, performing music, computer programming or even preparing a legal argument.

In fact, providing we are truly immersed in the activity, we can find flow in all sorts of places — for example cooking, yoga, painting, taking photos, gardening, reviewing contracts and writing.

A 10-year McKinsey study on the flow state found that top executives are up to 500 per cent more productive when they're in a state of flow. A complementary study by scientists at Advanced Brain Monitoring also found that being in flow cut in half the time it took to train novice marksmen up to an expert level.

But here's the thing. Most reports suggest that we can only spend about four hours in flow per day, and that the return on our time and energy begins to taper off fast after that—this is what's called the point of diminishing returns (see figure 3.1).

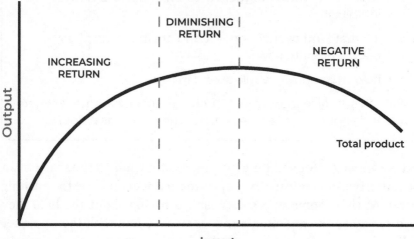

Figure 3.1: point of diminishing returns

GH Hardy, one of Britain's leading mathematicians of the first half of the 20th century, started his day with breakfast, checking the cricket scores and then settling in for a long day in the office: a long four-hour day, that is. From 9 am to 1 pm, he would be immersed in mathematics. The rest of the day, he busied himself with leisure activities like games of tennis and long walks in nature.

He told fellow Oxford professor CP Snow that 'four hours' creative work a day is about the limit for a mathematician'.

Charles Darwin too only worked about five hours a day, and that included a break for lunch. It didn't stop him from coming up with his ground-breaking theory of evolution.

A survey into the working lives of scientists carried out in the early 1950s arrived at the same conclusion. The data showed an M-shaped curve that rose steeply at first and peaked at 10 to 20 hours per week. Scientists working 35 hours a week were half as productive as their 20-hour-a-week colleagues. Not only does working long hours not make you more productive, but the lack of rest can harm the subsequent hours you spend in the office. This makes you less productive in the long-run.

To further this point, the 60-plus-hours-a-week researchers were the least productive of all.

Karl Anders Ericsson observed the same pattern in a study of violin students at a conservatory in Berlin in the 1980s.

According to Ericsson, 'deliberate practice is an effortful activity that can be sustained only for a limited time each day.' Practise too much, and you increase the odds of being struck down by injury or burning yourself out.

Students marked for greatness, they observed, had several short practice sessions each day, each lasting about 80 to 90 minutes, with half-hour breaks in between. The actual practice time added up to about four hours a day.

This upper limit, Ericsson concluded, is defined 'not by available time, but by available [mental and physical] resources for effortful practice'. After interviewing the students it became clear that 'it was primarily their ability to sustain the concentration necessary for deliberate practice that limited their hours of practice'.

This is why many executives report being more or less done by mid-afternoon, but almost as many nonetheless report staying in the office until mid-evening.

So maybe four hours a day of deliberate focus is all it takes. If it was enough for Charles Darwin, it might just be enough for you.

'Okay, Steve, I hear you. But how can we get focused in a world of constant interruption and distraction?!'

Getting into flow

The various means for getting into flow extend to a set of psychological, social and physiological 'triggers', which Steven Kotler of the Flow Genome Project, has popularised.

Psychological triggers

There are several psychological triggers that help propel us into the flow state.

Intense focus

Intense focus means no distractions, no multitasking, singular tasks and solitude.

I had the pleasure of speaking with Ben Mezrich for an episode of my *Future Squared* podcast. Mezrich has published 20 books, including a handful of *New York Times* bestsellers. Two of these, *Bringing Down the House* and *The Accidental Billionaires*, were adapted into the number one box office movies *21* and *The Social Network* respectively.

His writing process can only be described as manic. He wrote *Bringing Down the House*, a story about six MIT students who took Vegas by storm, in 14 days, and tends to write most of his books in just four to eight weeks.

He credits his prolific output to discipline, eliminating distractions and locking himself in a room with a clear and specific goal of writing six pages a day. And he doesn't stop for anything until those six pages are done. 'It could take two hours, or it could take all day.'

Clear goals

If we know what we're moving towards, we're far more likely to be motivated to get there than if we have no sense of direction or overarching vision.

This aligns with Edwin Locke's goal-setting theory of motivation. In the 1960s, Locke posited that goal setting is linked to task performance. In particular, Locke put forward the idea that specific, explicit and *challenging* goals, along with feedback, contribute to higher performance.

Goals give us direction about what needs to be done and how much effort is required.

Locke's team found that, as a result of setting goals, unionised truck drivers increased the number of logs loaded onto their trucks by 50 per cent, saving the company $250 000 in just nine months.

Immediate feedback

If you're not getting frequent enough feedback, you don't know if your actions are moving you closer to or further away from your goal. It's akin to driving blind: it's not much fun, and you're likely to crash.

Challenge-to-skill ratio

Research shows that when a task is a little beyond our current abilities, it requires us to strive, and is likely to get us into flow. When tasks are too easy, we get bored, and when they're too hard, we get discouraged.

So how much more difficult should the task be *exactly*?

Answers vary, but the general thinking is about 4 per cent. 'If you want to trigger flow,' Kotler says, 'the challenge should be four percent greater than the skills.'

Professional athletes get bored playing with amateurs, who themselves will be frustrated by the experience. There's an iconic photo of 5'3" Muggsy Bogues defending 6'5" Michael Jordan in the 1995 NBA Playoffs that demonstrates this point.

Note: On this occasion, the vertically challenged Bogues briefly stole the ball from Jordan before the referee called a foul on the latter for illegal contact. Check it out on YouTube (after you're done reading this chapter!).

High consequences

Risks keep us focused — or as Kotler puts it, 'uncertainty is our rocket ride into the present moment'.

When it's a matter of life or death, success or failure, there's no trying to get in the zone.

Alex Hutchinson, author of *Endure: Mind, Body, and the Curiously Elastic Limits of Human Performance*, shared some insights from Ross Tucker and his colleagues at the University of Cape Town on my podcast. They studied the average pacing strategies in men's middle- and long-distance track world records over the past century.

The patterns are remarkably consistent.

In the 5000 and 10 000 metres, the first and last parts of the race are the fastest. Of the 66 records set in the modern era in these two events, only once (Paul Tergat in 1997) has any kilometre other than the first or last been the fastest.

This tendency to speed up as we approach the finishing line is called 'the finishing kick'. It can be found not only in endurance sports, but also weightlifting and — if you look closely enough — the workplace and the classroom.

Take an example that we can all relate to: a high school essay. We may have procrastinated in the weeks leading up to the due date, but on the night or two beforehand, we suddenly found ourselves deeply immersed in finishing our essay.

These are examples of high consequences and time constraints propelling us into flow.

Rich environment

An environment with lots of changeability, novelty and complexity can focus our attention.

When we find ourselves in a new city or country, we tend to be much more present than we are when we're walking around our home neighbourhood. We pay extra attention to the sights and sounds that we'd otherwise filter out of our stream of consciousness. We spend less time daydreaming and listening to our internal narrative.

If you've ever been to the Las Vegas Strip, you'll know what an environment rich with lights, sights and sounds, along with desert heat, does for your sense of presence.

Social triggers

Given that social rewards and recognition from peers are salient motivators, it may come as no surprise to learn that there are several social triggers that serve to get us into the flow state.

Serious concentration

Doing something that requires serious concentration, such as playing chess or shooting a three-pointer, gets us into flow.

Larry Bird, three times NBA champion and MVP, knows a little about getting into flow.

Bird competed in the 1986 NBA All-Star three-point shootout contest. He established himself as soon as he entered the locker room before the shootout. He asked his competitors, 'Which one of you guys is going to finish second?'

He proceeded to participate in his warm-up jacket and dominated, scoring 22 out of a possible 30 points. This culminated with turning his back to the ring and raising a victorious index finger to the sky after the final basketball left his fingertips on its way to a swoosh. You don't do that without serious concentration, flow and a healthy dose of confidence.

He went on to become a three times three-point contest champion.

Shared, clear goals

When a US football team has called time out, is down by five points and needs a touchdown to win the game, with just five seconds on the clock, all of its players will be bound by a shared strategy locking them into the present moment.

As long as everybody knows what their job is, they will find themselves in flow, tuning out the roars of the crowd and focused on the task at hand.

If there is a hint of uncertainty or confusion about what a given player is supposed to do, this will prove devastating for the team. Fear will take over. Performing in a group situation requires the team to blend their egos — or what Kotler calls 'a collective version of humility' where no-one dominates the spotlight and everyone is involved.

Sense of control

This is where autonomy and mastery combine.

One of our fundamental human needs is certainty, or a sense of security and control. When we feel we are in control and the writer of our own stories, we are far more likely to pick up the pen than if somebody else is writing it for us.

When it comes to stress, we respond differently to heavy loads that we have elected to carry than we do to those that have been thrust upon us.

More broadly speaking, if we assume a victim mentality, there is no incentive to take action. If we assume a mindset of ownership and control, we empower ourselves to change our reality.

Close listening

This is about staying present when engaging in conversation and keeping your responses organic.

As 10-times NCAA winning basketball coach with UCLA John Wooden put it, 'We would be a lot wiser if we listened more. Not just hearing the words but listening and not thinking about what we're going to say.'

Having hosted the *Future Squared* podcast for several years and interviewed numerous thought leaders across myriad domains, I know that when I'm fully present in conversations, the quality of my questions and interactions with the guest benefit. When I let my presence slip, the conversation suffers.

Hosting interviews about topics I'm genuinely curious about but know little about has forced me to sharpen my listening skills and ask better questions.

By being totally tuned into the conversation, I can (try to) inject wit and interject at key moments. This makes for a much more enjoyable conversation for me, and, more importantly, for my listeners.

When I've had a great conversation, I ride the natural high that follows. It's a high that can last for hours, and it sets me up for a high energy day ahead, given that I record most of my podcast episodes before 8.30 am. I often like to schedule any sales calls I have to make after a podcast, so that I can put that positive energy and rhythm into those calls and increase my chances of getting prospects over the line.

If you're engaged in a conversation and you're just waiting for the other person to finish speaking so you can say what you want to say, you're hardly listening. Close listening—and the conversations that come from it—is far more rewarding than conversations where people essentially speak at each other and not with each other.

Always say 'Yes, and...'

In a team discussion or brainstorming session, do as the team from pre-eminent design thinking agency IDEO does, and practise saying 'Yes, and...'.

Your interactions should build upon the contributions of others, rather than oppose their ideas. This serves to build momentum and generate lots of ideas, which, after all, is the purpose of a brainstorming session. If we cut each other down at the first opportunity to criticise, it puts people on the defensive. It increases insecurity and puts a dampener on people's motivation to contribute.

You wind up with groupthink where the most dominant or highest-paid person's ideas are taken forward, regardless of their quality.

A word on HIPPOs: As long-time Google CEO and chairman Eric Schmidt wrote in *Trillion Dollar Coach*, 'A place where the top manager makes all decisions leads to just the opposite...In that scenario, it's not about the best idea carrying the day, it's about who does the best job of lobbying the top dog; in other words, politics.'

Pattern recognition

Pattern recognition involves linking ideas together organically.

At the 2005 commencement ceremony for students at Stanford University, the late Steve Jobs said, 'You can't connect the dots looking forward; you can only connect them looking backwards.'

You may have found yourself making connections between seemingly disparate ideas when you're hiking in nature, singing in the shower or lifting weights in the gym.

I experience this when making connections between something a podcast guest may be saying and something another guest may have spoken about previously: 'Oh, this aligns with something Adam Grant said about...'.

This is the essence of creativity: the intersection of disparate ideas. It's one of the reasons why the Renaissance was representative of such an artistic and cultural revolution in Italy from the 14th to the 17th centuries. As Frans Johansson wrote in his book *The Medici Effect*, the creative revolution was sparked by the patronage of the ruling Medici family. The family brought to Florence the best sculptors, architects, engineers, poets, scientists, philosophers and painters. The creative revolution happened at the *intersection* of all of these disciplines.

Interestingly, when it comes to pattern recognition, a full eight hours of sleep can go a long way. Approximately 75 per cent of our deep REM (rapid eye movement) sleep—critical for creativity and forming connections between disparate ideas—occurs between the sixth and eighth hours of sleep.

Taking risks

Have the courage to take risks, no matter how unlikely you think you are to succeed.

Research shows that you may have a predisposition towards or away from risk-taking. Depending on the context, this could help or harm you. The University of Sydney found that people with a more active amygdala (the almond-sized part of the brain chiefly responsible for detecting threats) are more likely to lean conservatively. People with less active amygdalae are more likely to lean liberally. See figure 3.2.

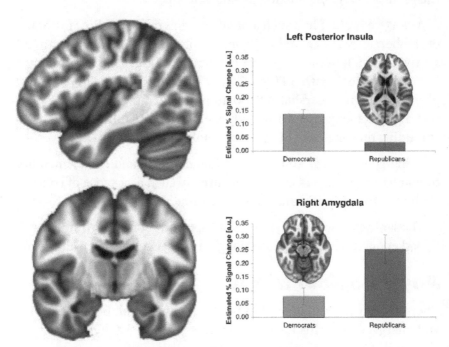

Figure 3.2: red brain, blue brain
Source: Schreiber D, Fonzo G, Simmons AN, Dawes CT, Flagan T, Fowler JH, et al. (2013) Red Brain, Blue Brain: Evaluative Processes Differ in Democrats and Republicans.

Furthermore, the latter are more likely to be predisposed towards entrepreneurship, as liberal thinkers tend to be more comfortable with the risks posed by ambiguity, while the former are likely to become managers of what already exists.

A sharpened sword

You can't get into flow if you're chopping onions with a blunt knife.

If you tried to learn the guitar as a child but you were given a cheap hand-me-down that sounded terrible, you would have been unlikely to find yourself getting into flow playing it. You probably found the opposite: frustration, culminating with your throwing the guitar on the ground and going outside to ride your bike.

As a 13 year old, I had such a hand-me-down. I recall how my hours of deliberate practice and enjoyment increased dramatically after I scraped enough money together (working at Target, no less) to buy a BC Rich Warlock with a Floyd Rose bridge and EMG 81/85 pickups, played through a Marshall VS100 amp (for the guitar enthusiasts). It was a gamechanger, and I quickly went from strumming ballads to shredding on songs like Megadeth's 'Holy Wars'.

Using 'good enough' equipment is foundational, and complementary to many of the triggers mentioned already such as a sense of control, challenge-to-skill ratio and rich environment.

The same extends to a good enough laptop, a good enough surfboard, a good enough wrench, a good enough internet connection, and so on.

Physiological triggers

There is a powerful connection between your mind, body, emotions and energy. Given this inextricable link, you can 'hack' your body to clear and engage your mind, and get into flow.

Meditation and mindfulness

Calm the mind, think clearly and stay present on the task at hand. 'Headspace', 'Calm' and Sam Harris' 'Waking Up' mobile apps are great places to start.

Binaural beats

First discovered in 1839 by physicist Heinrich Wilhelm Dove, binaural beats play different audio frequencies in each ear, which coalesce to trigger brain activity, getting you into the flow state. Try listening to some beats for free at myNoise.net and Brain.fm the next time you're doing something that requires full concentration.

On audio, Matt Mullenweg, founder of WordPress, says that listening to the same song on repeat gets him into flow. Arkansas psychologist Elizabeth Hellmuth Margulis echoed these thoughts in her book, *On Repeat: How Music Plays the Mind*.

Having said that, other studies have found that listening to music while working may actually be distracting—so try it out and see what works for you. It may come down to the nature of the work you're doing.

Smart drugs

Smart drugs are cognitive enhancers that support focus, memory, creativity and motivation—better known to Silicon Valley types as 'nootropics'.

Popular brands include Onnit's Alpha Brain, Bulletproof Coffee's Brain Octane, and Four Sigmatic's Mushroom Coffee. While writing this book, I invested in a nootropic called BrainX, which utilises several Brazilian herbs to improve drive, energy and focus.

Batch processing

As the title suggests, this is about doing things in batches.

Lifestyle entrepreneur and all-round motivational guru Tim Ferriss popularised this idea in his *New York Times* bestseller, *The 4-Hour Work Week*. The idea is that you select times of day to batch processes such as checking email. This way, you limit distractions and stop chasing shiny objects down rabbit holes.

★　★　★

Now that we've established how to get into flow, and why it is the key to doing your best work, we'll dive into the benefits of flow on your emotional wellbeing.

We'll also bust a little myth which posits that in order to be productive, you need to rise before the sun does.

CALL TO ACTION

Apply the following action items to spend more time in flow.

1. Incorporate as many of the flow triggers as you can into your work and life.

2. Determine which of your tasks you can batch (e.g. do once or twice a day), and then commit to doing so.

3. Check out Brain.fm, a 'flow' playlist on Spotify or listen to the same song on repeat, and see if this propels you into flow.

4. Try meditating to clear your head before working (Headspace, Calm and Sam Harris' meditation app Waking Up are good places to start).

5. Explore nootropics to see whether or not they give you a cognitive boost.

CHAPTER 4
Dr Feelgood

Getting into flow can improve emotional wellbeing and lead to a more happy and rewarding experience of life.

As Mihaly Csikszentmihalyi said in an interview for *Psychology Today*, 'Once you experience flow, you want to experience it again. You don't know why, but you know that when you are in that state of mind, you feel better than when you aren't.'

Csikszentmihalyi went on to say that people tend to take shortcuts to help them focus (including drugs and religious rituals) and that they soon realise that flow is one of the best ways to give yourself good feelings without depending on anything else to make it happen.

Unlike shallow-level work, studies have demonstrated a strong link between time spent in flow, also known as deep work, and a positive attitude, higher self-esteem and greater life satisfaction.

Csikszentmihalyi goes on to share that we should all ask ourselves what and who we like in this world and whether they make us better people.

He tells the story of having a hunting dog while living in Chicago. 'That dog was just a lump of flesh with no life in her. Except for the first time when I took her to the park, and she saw squirrels. She became careful, precise and elegant [at hunting]. She was very happy, even though she could never catch any squirrels.'

My proverbial squirrels are, among other things, hiking outdoors (as opposed to indoors, yes), surfing, deep conversations, keynote speaking, writing and getting out of my comfort zone. Want to live a more present and rewarding life? Catch more squirrels.

As Mithu Storoni, author of *Stress-Proof* wrote, 'This state of heightened mental alertness without negative emotional contagion is the holy grail of optimal performance, one that even manufacturers of smart drugs such as Modafinil and L-Theanine tend to aim for.'

BUILD ACTUAL THINGS WITH YOUR ACTUAL HANDS

In today's age, we can work around the clock. We might write books, develop software, record podcast episodes or deliver presentations. At its core, all we are doing is moving 0s and 1s around: it's all binary; it's all just code. It's not physically *real*.

The philosophers among you might be asking, 'Yes, but what is real, exactly?' and that, my friends, is beyond the scope of this book.

Recently, I decided to get in touch with my ancestral roots and build an actual thing with my actual hands.

As a huge fan of board sports, the actual thing in question was a skateboard.

The design was inspired by the *Cobra Kai* television series.

Building the board involved lots of small, incremental steps: picking out the parts and the design, stripping the original paintwork, sanding down the board, laying a base coat, printing and diligently cutting out stencils, spray painting designs onto the board and grip tape, cutting out and applying the grip tape, installing the hardware (trucks, bearings and wheels) and touching up the board.

In all, the project took me five weekday evenings to complete, but it was incredibly engaging and rewarding. There was something... primal about it, as if I was reconnecting with my ancestors, who were handy with a stone tool or two.

I wasn't checking my phone.

I wasn't watching Netflix.

I was in total flow, sometimes for several hours at a time, and it felt great—like I was operating from some higher level of consciousness.

And now I have something that I can actually point to in the physical world, and say, 'I built that'.

Not only that but 24 hours after having completed the project I was still buzzing.

The dopamine hit that comes with learning and building actual things, from being in flow, from revelling in the journey—not just the destination—is an immensely satisfying one.

And if you're thinking 'this guy has too much time on his hands', that's the whole point of this book!

Feelgood chemicals

When you're in flow, your brain releases five chemicals: anandamide, dopamine, endorphins, norepinephrine and serotonin. These aren't just any chemicals: these are performance enhancers that make us feel and perform better physically and mentally. Here's a run-down.

- Anandamide comes from the Sanskrit word *Ananda*, which translates to 'bliss'. It elevates mood, improves respiration, aids lateral thinking and inhibits fear. Jamie Wheal of the Flow Genome Project says the high that runners often experience is wrongly attributed to endorphins but is actually the work of anandamide. Interestingly, it is essentially a neurotransmitter that runs off the brain's cannabinoid system, and follows a similar pathway to that of marijuana.

- Dopamine is widely known as the feelgood or reward chemical. It's that feeling you get when you successfully nail a presentation you've been anxious about in front of a huge audience, or after you score a decisive goal on the soccer pitch. And it's not just the pleasurable act that brings us the chemical reward, but also the *anticipation* of a pleasurable act. Remember Pavlov's dog? It would start salivating as soon as it heard the bell it associated with feeding time. According to neuroendocrinologist Robert Sapolsky, it's not the reward but the anticipation that keeps the dopamine loop going. It's the planning and anticipation of a holiday, which can be just as rewarding, and in some cases more rewarding, than the holiday itself.

- Endorphins are your body's natural painkillers and pleasure pills. They are often likened to morphine! According to Katerina Johnson of the University of Oxford, endorphins are actually *stronger* than morphine, and her research team found that you can get more of them simply by having more friends.

- Norepinephrine enhances our focus and releases glucose into the bloodstream, boosting our energy, and increasing our arousal and emotional control. From a work perspective, this makes it easier for us to lock in on one thing, rather than check Twitter for the seventh time that morning.

- Serotonin is the mood regulator. Low levels of serotonin are linked with depression, while high levels of serotonin are linked with happiness, as well as social dominance. Psychologist and author of *12 Rules for Life* Jordan Peterson suggested, somewhat famously now, that lobsters, like most animals in the animal kingdom — including human beings — exist in hierarchies that run on serotonin. The higher up you are in the social hierarchy, the more serotonin you have available. The more defeat you suffer, the more likely you are to have your serotonin suppressed, and the less likely you are to climb the social ladder. When you feel down and out, your behaviours will follow suit.

Knowing this, you can hack your day. Do something that gets you into flow before a big sales call, for example, so you can bring heightened energy and confidence to the call, increasing your chances of success.

At its core, the flow state offers us a natural cocktail of feelgood, performance-enhancing chemicals. The more time we can spend in flow, the happier we'll feel, the better we'll perform and the further we'll get.

The downside? Like many drugs, legal or otherwise, the more you take, the more you need to take to stimulate the response. This is why making things progressively more challenging is one of the keys to stimulating flow. You might have enjoyed playing Deep Purple's 'Smoke on the Water' as a new 10-year-old guitarist, but it gets boring very quickly. At that point, it's time to progress to Zeppelin's 'Stairway to Heaven'.

Managing attention

Given all of this, it makes little sense to measure time instead of attention when it comes to heuristic tasks. You may spend 12 hours in the office but no time in flow at all, and walk away with little to show for it. Or you may spend just three hours in the office, in total flow the whole time, and create five times more value than the passive worker who complains proudly about just how busy they are whacking moles.

Killing night owls softly

Sir Richard Branson wakes up at 5 am every day. Jack Dorsey of Twitter, Square and Cash App fame is up at 5.30 am before walking eight kilometres to the office. About 90 per cent of executives identify as being early risers (some of them might just be signalling).

In reality, people get into flow at different times.

Science suggests that our preferred sleeping patterns — our chronotypes — are programmed at birth.

People are either night owls or early birds. Astrophysicist Sabrina Stierwalt wrote for *Scientific American* that

> our preferences [for one or the other] are encoded in genes called 'clock' or 'period' genes that regulate our circadian rhythms, and are thus linked to our blood pressure, metabolism, body temperature and hormone levels.

Sayings like 'the early bird gets the worm' and beliefs that successful people are early risers — glorified by the likes of ex-Navy SEAL Jocko Willink (who posts a photo of his wristwatch to Instagram at 4.30 each morning) — might actually have to do with the fact that the standard workday is better suited to early risers.

If the rules of the game are heavily skewed in favour of your biological predispositions, then you're more likely to win.

Stierwalt said that workdays usually start between 7 and 9 am. However, night owls can experience 'social jetlag' if they wake up this early — that is, they can feel like they would if they had jetlag after an overnight flight. Early risers are less likely to experience social jetlag, giving them an advantage over night owls.

Studies show that while early risers are more alert in the morning, night owls show stronger focus and longer attention spans 10 hours after waking than their early-bird compatriots.

A study published in the journal *Personality and Individual Differences* had researchers observing over 700 people who showed a split in personality traits between night owls and early risers. Early birds tended to be more persistent and resistant to frustration, and showed lower levels of anxiety. Night owls were braver, but more likely to develop addictive habits (this may be influenced by the many temptations of the night that aren't as evident or plentiful during the day).

Several studies have found that about 30 to 40 per cent of the population are night owls, which means that the modern 9-to-5 workday is sabotaging the creative and intellectual efforts of *almost half the workforce*. Perhaps it's sabotaging yours?

Diminished productivity might not be the only downside for night owls. They face a 10 per cent higher risk of early death than early birds, according to a study by Kristen Knutson published in *Chronobiology International*.

In his best-selling book *Why We Sleep*, Matt Walker finds that sleep deprivation shows a 60 per cent amplification in emotional reactivity. With a full night of plentiful sleep, we have a balanced mix between what Walker calls our emotional gas pedal (our fight-or-flight-inducing amygdala) and our brake (our prefrontal cortex). Without sleep, the strong coupling between these two brain regions is lost.

He tells us that healthy people can experience a neurological pattern of brain activity similar to depression, anxiety, post-traumatic stress disorder, schizophrenia and bipolar disorder if they have their sleep disrupted or blocked.

Insufficient sleep can also lead to an early onset of neurodegenerative diseases such as Alzheimer's due to a collection of amyloid beta plaques in the brain.

Successful night owls

While there's no shortage of heavy hitters glorifying the 5 am alarm clock, there are also examples on the other side of the spectrum.

Mark Zuckerberg told Jerry Seinfeld in a Facebook live Q&A that he normally gets up at 8 am.

BuzzFeed CEO Jonah Peretti routinely sleeps until 8.30 am.

The New Yorker journalist Kathryn Schulz told *Business Insider* that her writing brain kicks in at about 10 pm, so she does most of her writing in the wee hours of the morning.

Aaron Levie, CEO of billion-dollar cloud storage company Box, wakes up at 10 am.

Alexis Ohanian, founder of Reddit, author and husband to tennis superstar Serena Williams, says he normally hits the sack at 2 am and gets up at 10 am.

Meanwhile, legendary US author Hunter S Thompson would normally settle in to write at midnight, albeit in his case aided by a daily diet of burgers, drugs and alcohol.

Startup investor, entrepreneur and deep thinker Naval Ravikant said it well in an appearance on the popular *The Joe Rogan Experience* podcast:

> Machines should be working nine to five. Humans are not meant to work nine to five. It makes no sense to work nine to five, yet that is what we keep doing, despite the fact that it is working less and less.

He went on to say that work isn't linear and inputs don't result in the same outputs for every person.

Or, as Seneca put it almost 2000 years earlier, 'Our minds must relax: they will rise better and keener after a rest…unremitting effort leads to a kind of mental dullness and lethargy.'

We shouldn't feel demonised for getting up late, or working late. If you're going to demonise anything, let it be failing to live up to your potential, whether that be as an early bird or a night owl.

A word on passive leisure

People don't get into flow during passive leisure activities such as watching television or relaxing. Some passive activities even produce a state of mild depression. For example, when binge-watching a Netflix series, your brain can fall into a trance-like state—the alpha brain waves minus the benefit of the theta brain waves.

★　★　★

As we've explored, all kinds of activities can produce flow. It's important to engineer the conditions for flow into your everyday life as much as possible in order to lead a more rewarding and joyful life.

CALL TO ACTION

To spend more time in the flow state and do your very best work, take heed of the following.

1. Leave the office when you've hit the point of diminishing returns.

2. Engineer more flow triggers into your life.

3. Write down the kinds of activities that make you feel awesome and do more of them.

4. Take whatever action you can towards working in alignment with your chronotype.

PART 3
THE MODERN WORKPLACE

More often than not, when organisations underperform, it's not attributable to a few bad eggs but to a toxic culture that pervades the entire workplace.

In the following chapters, we will explore the myriad ways that organisations and people compromise their potential to do great things.

CHAPTER 5

How organisations kill productivity

As a child of the 1990s, I grew up watching an episode of *The Simpsons* each and every weeknight at 6 pm, usually during dinner.

In an episode called 'Bart on the Road', the motley crew of Nelson, Milhouse, Martin and Bart made their way to the World Fair in Knoxville, Tennessee. They were armed with nothing but a fake ID that Bart had ingeniously made, a wad of cash, a rental Oldsmobile and a 1982 AAA Guidebook.

As a 10 year old, it's about as much fun as you can imagine having! Except, there was one flaw in their plan. It was 1996, and the World Fair had long since shut down.

Bad things happen when you try to navigate a new world with old maps, but that's what most large organisations are doing today. They're navigating the world with factory floor norms of the early 20th century. Such norms extend to hierarchy, valuing physical presence and the 9-to-5 workday.

Niccolò Machiavelli put it well in *The Prince*, almost 500 years ago: 'A prince is successful when he fits his mode of proceeding to the times, and is unsuccessful when his mode of proceeding is no longer in tune with them.'

Flow killers in today's workplaces

Only 15 per cent of employees worldwide are engaged by their jobs—that is, only 15 per cent are emotionally invested towards delivering on their organisation's mission. Six out of seven people you see out on the city streets and in the workplace, are either not engaged or actively *disengaged*. Fancy most of the people in the world spending most of their time doing something that doesn't engage them. It's nothing short of a collective human tragedy.

In large part, this has to do with the fact that the modern organisation inadvertently sabotages flow and its people's potential by way of the following counterproductive practices and norms, which treat educated and capable adults like children:

- *availability:* an expectation that employees are always available
- *responsiveness:* an expectation that employees will respond immediately to internal and external correspondence
- *meetings:* an expectation that people should attend every meeting they're invited to.

So where do these norms come from?

Aside from apparent holdovers from the Industrial Revolution, a number of variables have coalesced to bring us to the present day.

Trusting one another

I had the pleasure of speaking with Jonathan Rosenberg and Alan Eagle, long-time senior Google executives and authors of *How Google Works* and *Trillion Dollar Coach*, the latter of which unpacks the leadership playbook of legendary Silicon Valley coach, Bill Campbell.

Campbell mentored the likes of Steve Jobs, Larry Page, Eric Schmidt and Jeff Bezos, among other tech luminaries, and played a major role in the success of their companies.

In order to empower great people to succeed, Campbell knew that an environment that liberates and amplifies their energy is critical. To do that, managers must support, respect and trust their people.

In order to develop that trust himself, Campbell would demonstrate a high level of vulnerability, much more than is typical in a business relationship. As a result of his openness, people would trust and mirror him, becoming more vulnerable themselves and creating space for a culture of transparency to emerge.

Humans need trust to flourish

As David Rose argues in *Why Culture Matters Most*, prosperity requires large group cooperation. This requires trust, but as societies grow larger this becomes more difficult to sustain.

Human flourishing, Rose argues, requires the general prosperity that comes from a free market system. Without trust, the foundations of the economy come crashing down. There is a danger of 'redistributive favouritism', which undermines trust in the system generally. This is manifest in inequality, political tribalism and left-leaning voices angrily calling for a redistribution of wealth due to a withering away of trust. This view was only hardened by the banker-instigated financial crisis of 2008.

Workplaces also need trust to flourish

Human beings are wired to be opportunistic, so if you find yourself with an opportunity that won't harm anybody, you'll likely take it. In a small group or tribe, we know that our actions might impact someone we know or care about. The harm becomes more real and visceral. Conversely, when we're in a large group, this disposition withers away, and we can much more readily find ourselves rationalising misconduct.

This is one of the reasons why large organisations are embroiled in policy and process, not just to keep the ship afloat, but to minimise misconduct, intentional or otherwise.

A 2014 report by Interaction Associates on trust in the workplace found that just four in 10 employees have a high level of trust in management and the organisation. Sadly, in stark contrast to the culture of trust that Bill Campbell sought to build, only 38 per cent of employees surveyed in the report said that they feel safe communicating their opinions with leadership. More than half don't trust their line manager.

Interestingly, high-trust companies are two-and-a-half times more likely to be high-performing organisations relative to 'trust laggards'. In an era of rapid change, this last statistic makes perfect sense. When things are changing faster outside your walls than inside your walls, innovation and adaptation become key. But if people don't trust each other, you end up with a gap between what people say, think and do.

Politics and consensus-seeking meetings take over, and organisational cadence grinds to a halt. You end up pushing away your best talent, and attracting people who like hiding behind policies and processes. Organisations can ill afford this in today's economy.

As Stephen Hawking purportedly said, 'Intelligence is the ability to adapt to change.' With 80 per cent of survey respondents reporting that a high level of trust fosters innovation, trust is one of the key ingredients behind building an innovative culture.

High stakes

As of writing, Fortune 500 companies represent more than US$1 trillion in profits, US$21 trillion in market value, and they employ about 28 million people globally.

It's easy to see why organisations put process in place when they have hundreds of millions in revenues, generous employee pay packets, customers who depend on them, shareholders to deliver returns to and regulation to comply with. Process ensures the smooth delivery of an existing and repeatable business model.

Such organisations can't afford to let avoidable screw-ups, such as privacy leaks, jeopardise their share price, which can see billions stripped from company valuations, and executive wealth, virtually overnight. For example, the Sony PlayStation Network privacy hack of 2011—which compromised 77 million accounts—cost the company an estimated $171 million.

Processes are supposed to help organisations scale, improve efficiency and minimise screw-ups. But like almost anything taken too far, they have unintended consequences.

When the same procedures bind both high- and low-risk activities, you have a recipe for disaster. It's akin to treating getting out of your car with the same vigour as jumping out of a plane — the result being that little meaningful work gets done.

I've had the joy of dealing with numerous large companies that take multiple weeks, multiple people and multiple sign-offs to raise a purchase order for a simple $9000 engagement. 'Will give you an update next week when we have more team members available to assist,' we're told. And I'm talking about companies with 10-figure revenues here. They've created full-time jobs out of moving paper from one desk to the next.

According to Boston Consulting Group, over the last 15 years, 'the amount of procedures, vertical layers, interface structures, coordination bodies, and decision approvals...[had] increased by anywhere from 50% to 350%'.

They also found that managers spend 40 per cent of their time writing reports and up to 60 per cent in coordination meetings.

SIMPLE SABOTAGE

On 17 January 1944, the Office of the Strategic Services of the CIA issued the *Simple Sabotage Field Manual*. The manual remained classified for decades, and was declassified in 2008.

The purpose of the manual was to present suggestions for inciting and executing sabotage.

The manual is full of 1940s references such as 'axis nationals', the latter's forces no doubt falling victim to many of the manual's methods.

What's striking about this section of the manual is that it sounds just like many of the dated management practices that plague organisations today. These practices continue to sabotage organisations when it comes to creating an environment where stuff gets done.

See table 5.1 (overleaf) for some excerpts from the manual and how they show up in organisations today. You'll no doubt draw parallels between these and the way many organisations operate today.

(continued)

SIMPLE SABOTAGE (*cont'd*)

Table 5.1: excerpts from the *Simple Sabotage Field Manual* (left-hand column) and how they show up in organisations today

Excerpt from *Simple Sabotage Field Manual*	How this shows up today
Insist on doing everything through 'channels'. Never permit short-cuts to be taken in order to expedite decisions.	Outsourced accountability Going through the appropriate channels for every decision, no matter how inconsequential Multiple levels of approval from different business units
When possible, refer all matters to committees, for 'further study and consideration'. Attempt to make the committees as large as possible—never less than five.	Steering committees Meetings with absolutely *everyone* around the table, even though only two or three people really need to be there, done for the purpose of outsourcing accountability in case something goes wrong Multiple hand-offs between business units, only serving to slow things down to a halt
Haggle over precise wordings of communications, minutes, resolutions.	Painfully slow morale-sucking haggling over tiny details by: • marketing and communications • middle managers • legal • and more
Refer back to matters decided upon at the last meeting and attempt to re-open the question of the advisability of that decision.	Meetings to prepare for meetings Meeting decisions that don't get actioned and get carried over into subsequent meetings

Excerpt from *Simple Sabotage Field Manual*	How this shows up today
Advocate 'caution'. Be 'reasonable' and urge your fellow-conferees to be 'reasonable' and avoid haste which might result in embarrassments or difficulties later on.	Fear of failure Trying to get things 'perfect' the first time, but getting analysis paralysis and moving too slowly instead
Be worried about the propriety of any decision—raise the question of whether such action, as is contemplated, lies within the jurisdiction of the group or whether it might conflict with the policy of some higher echelon.	We all know someone like this. It is usually the manifestation of insecurity and ego and a desire to avoid change and do as little work as possible
In making work assignments, always sign out the unimportant jobs first. See that the important jobs are assigned to inefficient workers of poor machines.	The modern worker has a tendency to do whatever is easiest first thing in the morning, when most people are at their best and freshest, and procrastinate when it comes to more difficult, important tasks, only getting to them when their cognitive faculties are nearing depletion for the day or when deadlines insist on it

(continued)

SIMPLE SABOTAGE (*cont'd*)

Table 5.1: excerpts from the *Simple Sabotage Field Manual* (left-hand column) and how they show up in organisations today (*cont'd*)

Excerpt from *Simple Sabotage Field Manual*	How this shows up today
Insist on perfect work in relatively unimportant products; send back for refinishing those which have the least flaws. Approve other defective parts whose flaws are not visible to the naked eye.	Treating simple prototypes like full-scale products Putting every little idea or test through a business case process Trying to get products that are ready for the market 'perfect' before release, resulting in analysis paralysis Not applying professional judgement when applying risk mitigation techniques to new ideas, instead opting to get 100 per cent of the information and mitigate 100 per cent of the risks, no matter how low the impact or likelihood, to an acceptable residual risk
Hold conferences when there is more critical work to be done.	I don't know about you, but to me it seems like a lot of conferences exist purely for the purpose of getting out of doing work
Multiply the procedures and clearances involved in issuing instructions, paychecks, and so on. See that three people have to approve everything where one would do.	Multiple levels of approval required to get anything done—one of the major barriers to innovation and job fulfilment at large companies today
Apply all regulations to the last letter.	'That's the way things have always been done around here!' Again, we all know someone like this in our organisations

Excerpt from *Simple Sabotage Field Manual*	How this shows up today
Apply all regulations to the last letter. (*cont'd*)	Approach them with a problem and they respond with process. This is also typical of the mentality of many a public servant
Work slowly. Think out ways to increase the number of movements necessary on your job: use a light hammer instead of a heavy one, try to make a small wrench do when a big one is necessary, use little force where considerable force is needed, and so on.	Many organisations are inadvertently making their employees work slower by rolling out Microsoft Surfaces. Yes, they're cool, but they're no laptop. Jokes aside, many of the processes and systems in place at large companies ultimately force employees to move at a much slower cadence than is necessary
Contrive as many interruptions to your work as you can: when changing the material on which you are working, as you would on a lathe or punch, take needless time to do it. If you are cutting, shaping or doing other measured work, measure dimensions twice as often as you need to. When you go to the lavatory, spend a longer time there than is necessary. Forget tools so that you will have to go back after them.	Interruptions don't need to be contrived at the modern workplace: • email and other desktop notifications • physical interruptions • smartphone notifications The modern office is plagued with an 'urgency' over importance bias that means deep work often plays second fiddle to fighting fires and responding to emails (or Facebook Messenger messages) Oh, and I'm sure we all know someone who takes one too many 'smokos' (a colloquial Australian term for a cigarette break) or seems to have what amounts to a seriously weak bladder

(continued)

SIMPLE SABOTAGE (*cont'd*)

Table 5.1: excerpts from the *Simple Sabotage Field Manual* (left-hand column) and how they show up in organisations today (*cont'd*)

Excerpt from *Simple Sabotage Field Manual*	How this shows up today
Give lengthy and incomprehensible explanations when questioned.	We all know a manager like this, right? Not fun to deal with when all you want is a sharp answer so you can get on with things. Sadly, this is often a result of our sense of self-importance, lack of self-awareness and an environment where transparency isn't encouraged The end result: an employee who doesn't ask as many questions as they should to either be their best or prevent mistakes from occurring

Source of excerpts: CIA, *Simple Sabotage Field Manual*

In the immortal words of the one and only George Costanza, companies would be well served to 'do the opposite' of whatever the manual suggests.

Process over progress

Here are just some ways that process compromises progress.

- *The need for approvals:* an unreasonable number of approvals are needed to get anything done, signalling a lack of trust.

- *A focus on process instead of people:* today, if you present a problem to a typical government employee, chances are they will respond with a process instead of a solution: 'Fill out these forms, and we'll get back to you within 14 to 28 business days.'

- *An overdependence on meetings:* it's just not true that every decision requires a meeting, yet you'd think that this is the case, given how business executives spend their time.

- *Not supporting team morale:* the best employees are motivated not only by extrinsic rewards like pay, but more so by intrinsic rewards like purpose, autonomy and growth. Inundating your best people with process leaves them disgruntled and far lesser versions of themselves.

Another reason for managerial tendencies to over-burden an organisation with process is because we're inclined to conflate hours worked directly with output—a holdover from the widget-counting Industrial Revolution.

Applying dated management literature to today's intellectual worker doesn't make sense.

Few organisations know this and act on it better than Netflix, as we'll see in the next chapter.

CALL TO ACTION

Help create a culture that empowers people, rather than sabotages them, by using the following action items.

1. Write a list of 'flow killers' at your organisation and take steps to change them, beginning with the ones that you have some agency over.

2. Is there a high level of trust at your organisation, and if not, what can you do to develop more trust?

3. Write a list of your company's inhibiting policies and procedures and propose leaner alternatives—again, starting with the ones you have some agency over.

CHAPTER 6
People over process

Netflix's core philosophy is people over process: 'We have great people working together as a dream team...with this approach, we are a more flexible, fun, stimulating, creative, collaborative and successful organization.'

Netflix pays at the top of the market, not just to attract the best people and reward them according to their efforts, but to stay lean and fast. This offers them a serious competitive advantage over organisations that need to call a meeting every time they are required to make what normally amount to inconsequential decisions.

Netflix concedes that in a fast-moving and volatile business environment, keeping process to a minimum and empowering people to move quickly will inevitably result in mistakes. But smart, self-disciplined, accountable people who move fast, can learn from these mistakes, pick up the pieces and move forward even faster. Over time, the gap between them and their forever-pontificating-around-a-boardroom-table competitors becomes huge — and this becomes evident in their company performance over time.

Aligning values

All of the world's investment in digital transformation projects, and employee wellness programs (like fancy yoga studios and on-site masseuses) won't matter one iota if there's values misalignment between the organisation and its people.

The reason why the Netflix philosophy works for them is not just because they can *afford* to pay at the top of market, but also because their people *believe in the mission* and are aligned with the values of the organisation.

The absence of alignment is like bringing two people together who have fundamentally different life philosophies with the aim of having them build a romantic relationship. It's probably not going to work.

Most decisions should be made quickly

This brings me to what Amazon's Jeff Bezos calls Type 1 and Type 2 decisions.

Type 1 decisions are big, hairy, irreversible and high stakes. They require careful consideration: think decisions about security protocols that protect the privacy of your customer data and mitigate the chances of a seven-figure privacy breach coming your way.

Type 2 decisions are reversible. If you screw up, you can make amends without too much, if any, harm having been caused: think the font used in a landing page you're building to test appetite for a new product. However, it's not uncommon in many organisations to wait several weeks for marketing to green-light the font, colour scheme, position of a button and so on, before a product team can perform any testing.

Whenever I have to deal with corporate communications or marketing liaisons for our client engagements, instead of waiting for their initial input, I have my team just go ahead and build what we have in mind. We then send it over, and they usually just insist on a couple of minor tweaks (usually to validate their positions). We make the changes and move on.

In one of his annual shareholder letters, Bezos wrote that 'As organizations get larger, there seems to be a tendency to use the heavy-weight Type 1 decision-making process on most decisions. The end result of this is slowness, unthoughtful risk aversion, failure to experiment sufficiently, and consequently diminished invention.'

Most of our decisions are Type 2 decisions, and they should be made quickly (see figure 6.1).

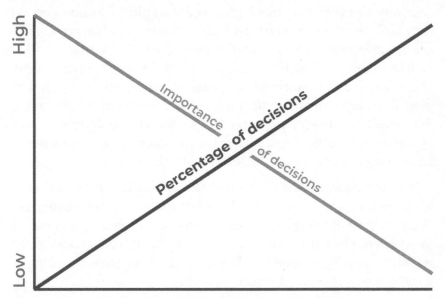

Figure 6.1: most decisions should be made quickly

Bezos, like any great thinker, advises being wary of the counterfactual. If we apply light-weight Type 2 decision-making to Type 1 decisions, we'll likely go extinct before we get large, he warns.

The trick lies in *knowing the difference*.

When it comes to Type 1 decisions, Bezos provides further guidance. At Amazon, they act once they have 70 per cent of the required information, instead of waiting for 90 per cent certainty. It's more effective to make a decision at 70 per cent certainty and course-correct than to wait for 90 per cent.

Disagree and commit

There may be all sorts of healthy and even fiery discussion when it comes to making a Type 1 decision. There should be. If it's a big, hairy, audacious, non-consequential decision, then you'll want people who may have different opinions to weigh in. You'll want to hear different perspectives, and work through the different permutations of outcomes. Agreeing may be a lot easier than conflict, but niceties have no place when you're making a decision about the future of the company. Conflict, communication and workplace dynamics expert Amy Gallo wrote in the *Harvard Business Review* that 'Disagreements are an inevitable, normal, and healthy part of relating to other people. There is no such thing as a conflict-free work environment. You might dream of working in a peaceful utopia, but it wouldn't be good for your company, your work, or you.' She went on to say that the benefits of disagreeing extend to better work outcomes as well as improved relationships, higher job satisfaction, opportunities to learn and grow and a more inclusive work environment.

Joel Garfinkle, author of *Difficult Conversations*, wrote that while it's natural to want to be liked, that's not always the most important thing. Instead of being liked, focus on giving and earning respect, he says. 'Even when the subject matter is difficult, conversations can remain mutually supportive. Respect the other person's point of view, and expect them to respect yours.'

Arguments have a place, so long as those arguments stay respectful and as rational as possible, and don't descent into emotional dogfights where nobody, least of all the organisation, wins.

When a decision is made, it's best that everybody *commits* to it, despite which side they took during the discussions. You're far more likely to have a positive outcome, even if it's not the most optimal decision, if everybody commits to learning from any failures and making it work, than if people actively sabotage the decision because it wasn't theirs. As Google's Jonathan Rosenberg says, 'You can make mistakes but you have to commit. You can't have one foot in and one foot out, because if you aren't fully committed then the people around you won't be either. If you're in, be in.'

Empower your team to make decisions

I had the pleasure of chatting with Paul Roos, Australian Rules premiership winning coach (Australia's equivalent of the Superbowl) for an episode of the *Future Squared* podcast, and we delved into numerous parallels between the business world and the athletic domain.

One thing that stood out was empowering teams to make decisions.

If leaders don't empower people to make decisions, bad behaviours will permeate, and the few decision-makers become bottlenecks.

Over time, this compounds and the organisation ends up attracting poor performers, while pushing away high performers who want to get stuff done.

Roos also touched on something that may not be so obvious: the more you make decisions, the better you get at making decisions. This ties in with the concept of 'automatism', which refers to our ability to perform complicated actions without conscious thought: think tying shoelaces, riding a bicycle or driving a car.

As a chess novice, it might take you a frustratingly long time (at least for your opponent) to make your move, as there's a whole lot of conscious thinking going into every move and deliberation about what the second or third order consequence of your move is. But as you play more, you develop an implicit awareness and your moves get faster. Your moves become automatic.

In one study, 100 university students participated in a typing test. They were shown a blank QWERTY keyboard and then given 80 seconds to write the letters down in their correct location. On average, participants typed 72 words per minute and had 94 per cent accuracy, hitting six correct keys per second!

This sharpening of implicit awareness or intuition is what you get the more you make decisions. The next time you're faced with a type of decision you've made before, you're far more likely to make it progressively quicker and quicker.

In saying this, there's a right time and a wrong time to trust your intuition.

When you (probably) shouldn't trust your intuition

'Trust your intuition.'

We hear it all the time from self-help gurus who have a tendency to make baseless statements in order to motivate (or rack up easy Instagram likes from similarly baseless thinkers).

Why?

Let's first define intuition: *The ability to understand something instinctively, without the need for conscious reasoning.*

Instinctively? *Innate, typically fixed patterns of behaviour in animals in response to certain stimuli.*

Therefore, our intuition is essentially a hard-wired response to external stimuli.

What influences our intuition

Several factors coalesce to influence the quality, or lack thereof, of our intuition.

Evolution

Our behaviour has evolved through natural selection. For example, our fight-or-flight responses were critical to our survival on the African savannah tens of thousands of years ago.

Genetics

Genetics shape our personality traits. Researchers have found links between our DNA and addiction, sexual orientation and anxiety.

For example, the SLC6A4 gene, involved in transporting serotonin around the central nervous system, can trigger the development of social anxiety disorders.

The brain

We've already established that brain function can influence, among other things, our appetite for risk. Similarly, activity in the ventromedial prefrontal cortex (vmPFC) and dorsolateral prefrontal cortex (dlPFC) can influence whether someone is more rational or emotional when making decisions. Many a successful person will tell you that delaying gratification is a key to success, and if your intuition is wired to make predominantly gut-reaction decisions, then it's hardly wise to listen to it.

Foetal conditioning

Our time in the womb can affect how we behave throughout life. For example, a study from the University of Edinburgh found that exposure of the foetus to excessive levels of cortisol — because of stressors in the carrying mother's life — can cause mood disorders in life, influencing decision making.

During birth, the baby's exposure to vaginal bacterial is believed to have positive long-term effects on their microbiome and health. Babies delivered by C-section are usually swabbed with vaginal fluids to offset the risk of health problems in later life.

However, the jury is out on whether the risk of health problems in later life is attributable to the lack of contact with vaginal bacteria, or the antibiotics administered to mothers delivering via C-section.

Microbiome activity

Your microbiome — the trillions of viruses, fungi, archaea and bacteria that live in the gut — has its own nervous system, the enteric nervous system (ENS). It is popularly referred to as 'the second brain' and it is engaged in bi-directional communication with the brain. It can ultimately influence how we feel and the decisions we make.

These relatively new revelations about our microbiome are one of the reasons why gut cleanses have become so popular as of late, as an unhealthy gut can ultimately make us feel sluggish, sick, and, worse still, could pre-empt neurodegenerative diseases and an early grave.

Trust your gut? Not when you've just eaten copious amounts of simple carbs.

Upbringing and past experience

Your experiences as an infant, toddler, child, teenager and, to a certain degree, adult, influence how you see the world and make decisions. For example, not getting the emotional support you innately craved as an infant might result in your becoming a 'stage-five clinger' as an adult. Conversely, it can also result in you subconsciously 're-enacting' your infancy and pushing people away when they get too close.

If your parents were overbearing, you may become what psychologists call 'enmeshed' and desire unrestrained freedom as an adult, finding it difficult to commit to any one person, job or place of abode.

As Dr Connson Chou Locke of the London School of Economics put it in the *Harvard Business Review*, 'Intuition is essentially a feeling, and it may be that our aversion to a particular option is reflecting a hidden nervousness, insecurity or fear of the unknown. If so, then our intuition will lead us to reject a perfectly good option.'

Intuition and primal instincts may tell a neglected infant male to seek out many female bedmates as an adult, but if their overarching priority is to start a family, then acting on the impulse will prove their undoing.

Current environment

Our current environment, with all of its stimuli — time pressure, light, sounds, sights, temperature, our monkey brains, other people — can influence our decision making, so much so that if we were forced to make the same decision tomorrow, with a different set of stimuli, we might take a different path.

'Oh, what the hell, put it all on black!'

This is why author Robert Greene suggests increasing your reaction time in the face of external stimuli, allowing the emotional cobwebs to clear to make more rational decisions instead of ones you'll live to regret.

Time of day or month

We can extend the current environment to the time of day you make a decision. The chemical makeup in your brain and your mood will differ at different times of the day—this's why it's easier *not* to reach for that bag of Doritos at 11 am, but not so easy when you're stretched out on the couch watching a Kevin Hart Netflix special at 10 pm after a long day of making decisions.

See melatonin levels in males and females throughout the day in figure 6.2. In this instance, making decisions between 8 pm and 8 am is not advised as we're fatigued, sluggish and more inclined to be irritable.

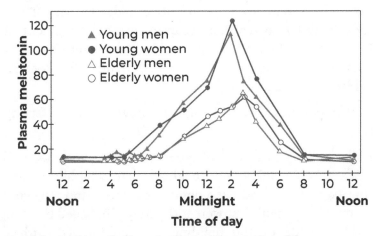

Figure 6.2: melatonin levels throughout the day
Source: Dean, W., Morgenthaler, J., & Fowkes, S. (1993). *Smart drugs II*. Petaluma, California: Smart Publications.

Fatigue is responsible for 20 to 30 per cent of fatal road accidents...and I'm only talking about melatonin here. I've not even considered the varying levels of dopamine, oxytocin, serotonin, anandamide, aspartate, glutamate, norepinephrine and other chemicals that can have a profound impact on our moods and decisions.

Still want to trust your intuition?

The quality of our intuition is limited by the experiences of our distant ancestors, our younger selves and our experiences throughout life.

These experiences might help us make good decisions in some instances, but not most.

In fact, most of us — insofar as our adult lives are concerned — have reasonably narrow experiences, and deep expertise in maybe one or two areas. We haven't invested the amount of time required to have developed trustworthy intuition in other areas.

So how long do we need to develop trustworthy intuition?

One study has found that it takes 10 years.

According to Dr Connson Chou Locke, writing in the *Harvard Business Review*, 'It takes a surprising amount of domain-specific expertise to develop accurate intuitive judgments...a TV show producer, in order to develop accurate intuitive judgment about new TV shows, would need to repeatedly engage in making decisions about new TV shows and receive rapid and accurate feedback [about the quality of those decisions].'

This also assumes that there are no moving parts affecting TV shows.

I'm sure the management of companies like Blockbuster, Toys 'R Us, Sears, DEC, Nokia and Kodak — and incidentally, numerous TV show executives — had deep domain expertise and trusted their 'professional judgement', but were ultimately blindsided by changing conditions outside of the building that culminated with their company's demise.

The same applies to your intuitive decisions: what factors are changing that could influence the outcome of your decision that you may or *may not* be aware of?

THE NARRATIVE FALLACY

Most business and personal development books fall victim to the narrative fallacy.

We have a tendency to associate a quality outcome with the quality of the decision and downplay the role of luck or mistakes. Just because you got lucky betting on black the first time, and your dopaminergic chemical reactions are telling you to bet the house this time, it's probably not a wise choice.

If we've made it in the business world, we'll look back through rose-coloured glasses and tell everyone about the linear, deliberate path we took to get to where we were, perhaps recounting the steps taken on a podcast, and forget about all of the setbacks, sleepless nights and serendipity along the way—as well as all of the factors we were blind to as illustrated in figure 6.3.

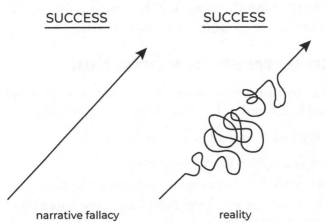

SUCCESS   SUCCESS

narrative fallacy   reality

Figure 6.3: what success really looks like

This is why one should always tread carefully when it comes to any sort of mentor–protégé arrangement, not only because we will overplay some contributing factors and discount others, but also because every scenario is different and what worked, when it worked for them, might not work for you.

And what about all those times your intuition abandoned you?

When it told you to throw a punch and you ended up getting your butt kicked?

Or that time it told you to hit on that girl, and she embarrassed you in front of all of your friends?

Or that time you felt compelled to take the game-winning shot and got nothing but...air?

(Of course, none of these examples were inspired by personal experience, in case you were wondering!)

'When you meet the right person, you will just know it.'

Will you?

How many of us have met somebody we thought was just perfect, Mr or Miss Right? We confessed our love to them, only for things to go downhill fast shortly thereafter? How many of us have looked back on said person and thought, 'What *was* I thinking?!'

When to trust your intuition

Of course, there are times when you should trust your gut, which is why I said in my earlier heading, 'When you (probably) shouldn't'.

You might want to trust your intuition when:

- you've got deep domain experience
- you've made similar decisions many times before
- consequences aren't significant and/or you don't have enough time to rationalise.

For everything else, you'll want to both *challenge* and *augment* your intuition.

Challenge your intuition

As Eugene Sadler-Smith and Erella Shefy wrote in their article, 'The Intuitive Executive: Understanding and Applying "Gut Feel" in Decision Making', 'Play devil's advocate. Test intuitive judgments; raise objections to them; generate counter-arguments; probe how robust your gut feel is when challenged.'

Augment your intuition

To augment your intuition:

- collect quantified data and apply reason
- seek input from several trustworthy and credible people with experience in the decision's domain.

When I'm making business decisions of significant consequence, I will 'work alone together' (more on this in chapter 12) with credible people to eliminate groupthink, mitigate my own biases and offset any lack of experience.

Logic isn't enough

You might think that I'm a stickler for reason and logic by this point, but ...

We can't make decisions *without* emotions. Neuroscientist Antonio Damasio studied people with damage to the emotion-generating part of the brain. They all seemed normal but what they had in common was that they *couldn't* make decisions. They found it difficult just to decide what to eat!

Optimal stopping

Finally, if you've augmented your intuition and still find yourself pontificating over which path to take, you might want to apply the mathematical theory of optimal stopping, or 'the 37% Rule'.

As Brian Christian, author of *Algorithms to Live By*, told me,

If you want the best odds of getting the best apartment (for argument's sake), spend 37 per cent of your apartment hunt (11 days, if you've given yourself a month for the search) noncommittally exploring options. Leave the cheque book at home; you're just calibrating. But after that point, be prepared to immediately commit—deposit and all—to the very first place you see that beats whatever you've already seen.

In a world of infinite options and variables impacting the quality of our decisions and eventual outcomes, it's almost impossible to make a 'perfect' decision, and even if we enjoy a positive outcome, we won't know what the alternatives could have been—so don't stress.

We can only ever optimise for 'most right' with the evidence at our disposal.

Once we've made a decision, we should commit, because by committing and investing energy into our decisions we are far more likely to succeed and reap the rewards—regardless of what the quality of that initial decision might have been—than if we go in half-hearted.

If self-help gurus were honest, they'd say 'challenge your intuition, use quantitative data, leverage credible people, and then commit to a decision'...but of course, that doesn't really work as an inspirational Instagram post.

If we respect and trust our colleagues—because arguably, that's why they were hired—shouldn't we be empowering them to be their best, and therefore, help our organisations reach new heights? Instead, we're bogging great minds down in process and policy that, rather than serving a purpose, ultimately leaves the vast majority of people feeling disengaged and disgruntled.

In the next chapter, we consider what the typical workday looks like for today's employees—and it's not pretty.

CALL TO ACTION

Here's how to put people over process in your organisation.

1. Stop treating all decisions as if they are Type-1 decisions.
2. Disagree and commit more.
3. Get better at knowing when to trust your gut, and when you should seek out data and the professional judgement of other people.
4. Practise 'optimal stopping' when presented with an overwhelm of options.

CHAPTER 7
The typical workday

As a result of the low-trust, high-process, slow-decision-making environment most organisations find themselves in, today's typical employee day is characterised by:

- hour-long meetings, by default, to discuss matters that can usually be handled virtually in their own time
- unplanned interruptions, helped in no small part by open-plan offices, instant messaging platforms, and the 'ding' of desktop and smartphone notifications
- responding to requests in a way reminiscent of Pavlov's salivating dog
- unnecessary consensus-seeking for reversible, non-consequential decisions
- rudimentary and administrative tasks
- travelling, often long-distance, to meet people face-to-face, when a phone call would suffice (if you travel to another city for a one-hour meeting, then it's not a one hour meeting, it's more like a 10+ hour investment of time and energy—not to mention, money).

Hyper-responsiveness

In a highly competitive job and business economy, it's easy to understand why people think they need to respond to requests from their boss or client in real time. They conflate it with meeting expectations. But there's a better way to meet expectations: deliver value. Paradoxically, to do that well requires you to be less responsive and more immersed in your work.

In most cases, it's just not true that bosses or clients demand an immediate response. Few things are needs. Responding immediately says more about us, our insecurities and our inability to prioritise our time than it does about them. If we are confident about the value we deliver, then we'll focus on delivering value instead of playing charades.

VALUES ALIGNMENT

Recently, I received a request for proposal (RFP) from a financial services organisation looking to run a corporate-startup partnership program.

Here's an example of the kinds of artefacts requested:

1. Quality control systems

2. Ability to report on service trends and spend analysis

3. Occupational health and safety policies

4. Sexual harassment policy

5. Diversity policy

6. Privacy policies, including non-disclosures and guarantees of employee confidentiality

7. Proof of ability to implement deliverables, including indicative timelines

8. Hours of operation, including after hours and support contacts

9. On-premise moustache curler available at all times.

What this signals is that this organisation:

» is not ready to work with startups

» is not ready for the fast-changing and increasingly uncertain realities of the 21st century, which call for flexibility and adaptability

» is not aligned with our values and would be a gigantic pain to work with.

I told them as much and moved on. No amount of money is worth compromising your values for.

Reply All

Reply All is a relic of a consensus seeking culture. We want to make sure *everybody* has received the correspondence in question so that should something go wrong, we can say, 'but you were cc'd in that email'. There are instances when Reply All makes sense, but they're the exception to the rule. More often than not, it's the wrong move because it harms everybody's productivity.

A 2018 Adobe study found that email and the instant messaging platform Slack costs companies US$28 209 per employee, per year.

Reply All only adds to the mental workload. It means employees have to scan and purge emails that aren't relevant to their work, taking time and attention away from more important priorities. It means they need to make countless more micro-decisions, which slowly eats away at their ability to make good decisions when needed.

It also adds significant direct costs by way of its impact on technology. For example, email traffic was delayed at Wells Fargo because of an accidental Reply-All chain involving 90 000 employees. It resulted in the backup of millions of emails and affected time-sensitive financial transactions.

Brunello Cucinelli, dubbed the king of cashmere by *The New Yorker,* says that at his company, emails can't be sent to more than two people. Echoing my sentiments on sharing the blame, Cucinelli says 'Why must a single email be ready by 10 different people, unless it's the 10 people who are interested in that specific issue? In order to disperse responsibility?'

Meetings and interruptions

When you pull someone out of their work to attend a meeting, you're not only disturbing their flow, but also incurring a steep opportunity cost, especially if meetings represent a significant part of your company culture.

I SAW THE SIGN

As for interruptions, if somebody is in flow and deeply immersed in a task, I won't interrupt them. But you might be thinking, 'How do I know if someone is in flow? It's not like I can read their brain waves!' Brainwave sensing headbands aside, we simply use props to help signal to the rest of the team if we are in flow. It could be that your headphones are plugged in, or that you've got a sign on your laptop monitor that says 'Do not disturb, I am surfing with aliens right now', or that you have a 'Santa's little helper' hat on, so long as the rest of your team knows what that means. They can send you a message via Slack instead, and leave you with more time in flow.

Jason Fried, co-founder of Basecamp and author of *It Doesn't Have to Be Crazy at Work*, said on the *Future Squared* podcast that for creative jobs such as programming and writing, people need time to truly think about the work that they're doing. If they don't get a good four hours of flow per day, he said, more hours won't make up for it.

Dominic Price, the resident work futurist at enterprise software company Atlassian, suggests cancelling all of your meetings. He told the *Australian Financial Review* that

meetings can kill my productivity,...my time investment, but they can also kill my job satisfaction. My time was this precious resource that I was frittering away on stuff that wasn't important or impactful. But no one else was going to change that unless I chose to change it.

He says that most meetings are boomerangs or sticks: either they come back when you throw them (you get invited again) or they don't come back. It turns out that two-thirds of his meetings were sticks and one-third came back. Like the team at Basecamp, he wanted to know his role, the purpose of the meeting and what he'd be held accountable for. As a consequence, he won back 15 hours a week to invest in more rewarding pursuits.

And worst of all, come the end of the day they often have little to show for it except anxiety, stress and an ever-mounting workload.

Workplace stress and mental health

It's probably not surprising to read that workplace stress is at a high.

But, what is stress?

The American Psychological Association puts forward three types of stress:

- *acute:* the most common, infrequently occurring and briefest form of stress, often caused by reactive thinking
- *episodic acute:* frequent, acute stress, experienced by Type-A personalities with an appetite for control, and perennial worriers
- *chronic:* the most harmful type of stress on physical and mental health. Repeated abuse in any form; unemployment, dysfunctional family, poor work environment, substance abuse or an unhappy marriage can cause significant chronic stress.

We've established that a little acute stress can be a good thing insofar as triggering flow is concerned. But when stress exceeds a healthy threshold, it becomes episodic acute stress, or worse still, chronic stress.

According to the National Institute for Occupational Safety and Health (NIOSH):

- 40 per cent of workers say that their job is very or extremely stressful
- 25 per cent view their job as the number one stressor in their lives
- 26 per cent say that they are 'often or very often burned out or stressed' by their work.

Stress shows up in different ways.

Psychological symptoms include depression, anxiety, irritability, pessimism, feelings of overwhelm and diminished cognitive functioning.

Behavioural symptoms extend to absenteeism, aggression, diminished initiative, problems with interpersonal relationships, disinterest, impatience and isolation.

Signs of stress are not always so obvious, with passive symptoms including criticising, disagreeing and procrastinating.

The financial cost

While the exact number has been contested, The American Institute of Stress estimates that job stress costs US companies more than US$300 billion a year in 'absenteeism, turnover, diminished productivity, and medical, legal and insurance costs'.

The physical cost

A team of researchers from the University of Medical Sciences in Iran set out to review the impact of stress on body function.

They found that stress impacts memory, cognition, mood, the immune system, our propensity to develop cardiovascular disease, gastrointestinal complications, inflammation and eating disorders, among other things.

But perhaps worst of all, stress can lead us to an early grave.

Stanford professor and author of *Dying for a Paycheck*, Jeffrey Pfeffer, suggests that workplace stress is the fifth biggest killer in the United States. He reported that workplace stress is associated with 120 000 US deaths per year and approximately 5 to 8 per cent of annual healthcare costs.

CEO of Barry-Wehmiller, Robert Chapman, went as far as saying that the audience was the cause of the healthcare crisis, when standing in front of 1000 other CEOs.

The human cost

Financial and physical costs aside, the real cost of workplace stress is the human cost. The cost to our personal creativity, our personal relationships, our attitude towards life and our energy to actually live the days we've been given.

Collectively, the cost on not just the stressed, but their families, communities and humanity as a whole can't be understated. Just imagine what the 55 per cent of Americans who report feeling stressed 'a lot of the day' could achieve if they weren't battling their internal demons all the time — not to mention the rest of the world's stressed-out citizens.

So, why are we so stressed?

The NIOSH report found three key reasons:

1. *workload:* so much to do, so little time to do it
2. *people issues:* navigating human behaviour and office politics
3. *work–life balance issues:* not having enough time to invest in personal relationships and life more broadly.

The report echoes Pfeffer's findings that workplace exposures negatively impacting human health include:

- working long hours in a week
- facing family-to-work and work-to-family conflicts
- facing high job demands such as pressure to work fast
- having relatively low control over your job and job environment.

Other stressors also extend to job insecurity, changes to duties, monotony, insufficient skills, micromanagement, inadequate resources, few growth opportunities, harassment and poor relationships with colleagues.

The NIOSH report highlighted the following organisational hygiene factors that manifest in the above:

- *the design of tasks:* heavy workload, long hours, few breaks and shift work; monotonous tasks with little sense of control
- *management style:* centralised decision making, sub-optimal communication and a lack of consideration for one's personal life.

A lack of control is one of the key contributing factors to workplace stress. Recently, researchers documented how essential a sense of control is for mind and body alike. In fact, some psychologists have gone as far as saying that the deepest need people have is for a sense of control.

Control is precisely what so many employees today don't have. They've become accustomed to colleagues snapping up time in their calendars, dragging them to meetings and ultimately having all sorts of non-consequential decisions go before a committee for review and worst of all, most just accept the status quo.

QUESTION TO PONDER

If you value your time at $100 an hour, but routinely work late, would you pay your company or your boss $400 to leave at 5pm instead of 9pm? If not, why do you do the same thing with your time which, unlike money, you can never earn back once it has been spent?

Feedback loops

A 'feedback loop' refers to the outcome of an action returning as a decision-making input. For example, if the outcome of my shooting a basketball is an air ball, that air ball also becomes a decision-making input: shoot the ball harder next time.

A short feedback loop is key to maintaining a sense of control. The longer the feedback loop, the lower our sense of control.

A feedback loop essentially has four discreet stages:

1. *data*
2. *information:* data becomes contextually useful information
3. *consequence:* information illuminates one or more paths ahead
4. *action:* recalibrate, decide and execute.

It can be positive, in which case you know you're on the right track, or it can be negative, in which case you know you need to change something.

But a long feedback loop renders us unable to see the paths ahead and confidently take action. It leaves us feeling unmotivated because we're not seeing any forward progress — we're just toiling away for what might seem to be ad infinitum.

Stanford psychologist and pioneer in the study of motivation Albert Bandura observed that giving individuals a clear goal and a means to evaluate their progress towards that goal greatly increased the likelihood that they would achieve it.

Edwin Locke also echoed these ideas, suggesting that better and appropriate feedback directs employee behaviour and contributes to higher performance than the absence of feedback. Feedback is a means of gaining reputation, making clarifications and regulating goal difficulties. It helps employees to work with more involvement and leads to greater job satisfaction.

THE POWER OF SHORT FEEDBACK LOOPS: WINNING DOGFIGHTS

The power of short feedback loops shows up across almost every domain, from business and athletics to military strategy.

It was US fighter pilot and leadership strategist John Boyd who coined the term OODA: observe, orient, decide and act.

During the Korean War, US fighter pilots flew F-85s, which on paper were inferior to the Soviet-issued MiGs that the North Koreans flew. But there were two crucial differences.

The F-85 featured a 360-degree bubble canopy, for better vision, and a fully hydraulic throttle, for better manoeuvrability. These two factors combined to shorten the US's feedback loop dramatically. When all was said and done, the Americans won the battle in the skies 10 to one.

When it comes to long-term projects, like building a startup, it can be tempting to default to the big IPO or private sale being the goal. But it can take most venture-backed startups eight to 10 years to get to that point (about 60 per cent don't). This is why Scott Belsky of Behance supplemented his team's goals with incremental goals, or surrogate goals, he formulated out of the blue. It's critical that you celebrate small wins, he stresses, but that you don't celebrate fake wins at the expense of hard truths.

For example, getting some media play might be nice, but if your leading indicators such as website visits, returning visitors and advertisement click-rates are all dropping fast, you should probably divert your attention accordingly.

Burnout

The term 'burnout' was coined by psychologist Herbert Freudenberger in the 1970s:

> If you have ever seen a building... burned out, you know it's a devastating sight... some bricks or concrete may be left; some outline of windows... the outer shell may seem almost intact. Only if you venture inside will you be struck by the full force of the desolation.

Someone who's burned out may not seem that way on the outside, but on the inside they are empty.

Burnout isn't just a byproduct of working too much; it's more complicated than that.

Researchers break burnout down into three parts:

1. *exhaustion:* becoming physically drained
2. *cynicism:* lacking engagement in your work
3. *inefficacy:* lack of belief in an ability to perform.

When we're burnt out, we become irritable, and our sleep, immune system and ability to focus suffer.

Long feedback loops and an office where it is almost impossible to get things done are key contributors to all of these factors.

Physical consequences of stress and burnout

The consequences of this go far beyond just productivity, and extend to physical and psychological disorders.

Jeffrey Pfeffer conducted a study that assessed the incremental annual healthcare costs incurred by employers based on different workplace conditions. The largest excess healthcare costs were due to job demands, with a total of US$46 billion in annual excess healthcare costs. Compare this with work–family conflict at US$24 billion, long work hours US$13 billion and low job control US$11 billion.

ARE YOU BURNED OUT?

The Maslach Burnout Inventory (MBI) is a leading burnout measurement survey and it addresses three general scales:

1. Emotional exhaustion

2. Depersonalisation—an impersonal response towards recipients of your service

3. Personal accomplishment—feelings of competence and successful achievement.

To determine if you're burned out, visit bit.ly/stanfordburnouttest

---

The paradox of performance

It's an obvious fallacy that companies must put pressure on employees to stay competitive and profitable. Research is now challenging this flawed notion.

Stressful working conditions result in absenteeism, low quality work and high employee churn. The latter can cost organisations upwards of $50 000 per employee when you consider costs associated with recruitment, onboarding, training and lost productivity.

Paradoxically, as we saw with Ford in 1914 (see chapter 1), building a more humane organisation characterised by shorter days and manageable workloads can have a positive effect on the bottom line. Microsoft Japan's 2019 4-day workweek experiment also delivered a 40 per cent increase in productivity.

A report by the National Institute for Occupational Safety and Health (NIOSH) found that the following factors are associated with low-stress work and high levels of performance:

- recognising employees for their performance
- offering employees career-development opportunities
- ensuring the organisational culture values individuals
- aligning management's actions with the organisation's values.

STRESS IN HOSPITALS

The St. Paul Fire and Marine Insurance Company conducted several studies on the stress-prevention programs in hospitals.

The studies looked at educating employees on stress-management, redesigning policies and procedures to address common causes of workplace stress and the establishment of employee assistance programs.

They found that the frequency of medication errors fell by 50 per cent after stress-prevention activities were implemented. In another study, malpractice claims fell by 70 per cent across 22 hospitals that implemented the activities. Worth noting, there was no decrease in malpractice claims in a comparison group of 22 hospitals where stress-prevention activities were not implemented.

Good stress

Acute stress comes with a higher sense of consciousness and as such, it can improve our performance on tasks such as giving a talk, taking a test or catching a wave.

As Dr Emeran Mayer wrote in his book *The Mind–Gut Connection*, flow benefits gut health by strengthening our defences to gut infections. This works in multiple ways. Acute stress increases acid production by the stomach in response to stress-related brain signals, making it more likely that invading microbes will be killed before they reach our intestines. It increases the secretion of antimicrobial peptides.

It also tells the intestines to increase fluid secretion and excrete contents, including pathogens (maybe this is why people often have to visit the toilet before partaking in a big event—kind of like Adonis Creed asking Rocky to remove his gloves before a big fight in the movie *Creed!*).

All these responses, Mayer says, defend the integrity of the gastrointestinal tract against potentially dangerous invaders and infection. He says that signals associated with happiness may increase gut microbiome diversity, improve gut health and protect us from infections and other diseases.

So what does this have to do with performance?

What we feel in our gut will ultimately affect not only the decisions we make about what to eat and drink, but also the people we choose to spend time with. It can influence the way we assess critical information such as workers, jury members and leaders.

This then becomes a virtuous cycle.

We perform better, we feel better, we invest more into our work, we continue to perform... and the virtuous cycle goes on. The value of incorporating as much flow as possible into our lives, and the value of the journey and who we end up being as a result, can't be overestimated.

★　★　★

We began this chapter with several flow killers. These included availability, responsiveness and meetings.

We've learned that these are all very much a by-product of 20th-century factory floor thinking, a lack of trust in our colleagues, burdensome processes and the high-stakes nature of the modern organisation.

We've also learned that this is having a devastating effect on the health of our people. So, why do we keep doing it?

It becomes apparent that organisational re-design can be implemented to mitigate unhealthy forms of stress. This has the potential to exponentially improve performance and make organisations more adaptable in an age when they have no other choice but to adapt.

In the next chapter, we'll explore the myriad ways your organisation can go about re-designing its environment to best support its people.

CALL TO ACTION

Create a workplace where people have more freedom and control by adopting the following action items.

1. Introduce signals to indicate when someone is in flow (or trying to be) and stop interrupting them when they are.

2. Stop scheduling one-hour meetings by default (15 to 30 minutes should do in most cases; a quick phone call or IM might suffice too—or maybe take ownership: make a Type-2 decision and get on with it!).

3. Shorten whatever feedback loops are apparent in your work.

4. Recognise colleagues for their performance.

CHAPTER 8
How to build a time-rich culture

'It's a necessary evil.'

These were the words of a former manager of mine at a leading Australian bank.

I had asked why 12 people had to be present for a three-hour-long meeting when 10 of them each had no more than five minutes of worthwhile contributions to make.

Her answer left me deflated.

Surely six-figure earning MBA graduates at one of Australia's top dealmakers would apply a little more critical thinking than what her response suggested.

But no.

Even before I had gone down the productivity rabbit hole that has culminated with my writing this book, I knew that her response had more to do with institutional conditioning than it had to do with reality. I knew that there had to be a better way.

I promised myself years ago to not blindly default to cultural norms that make no sense, whether in a professional setting or otherwise.

At Collective Campus, I've worked to build not only a culture where norms are challenged, but one where I'm actively challenged.

Our six-hour workday experiment and my subsequent *Harvard Business Review* article are testament to this philosophy.

The supposedly 'necessary evil' that is ineffective meetings was estimated to cost US organisations alone US$399 billion in 2019. Sadly, it's just one of many ways that organisations continue to waste their and their workforce's potential.

Fortunately, there are many things leaders can do to serve their people rather than sabotage them.

Minimum viable bureaucracy

As Machiavelli put it, 'A large body of infantry is impossible to feed and a small one insufficient to make a mark.'

As such, organisations should strive to optimise the size of project teams. They should be large enough to create impact, but not so large that they require countless paralysing processes just to keep everybody on the same page.

To help people escape the process paralysis introduced in chapter 3, opt for what agile practitioners call a minimum viable bureaucracy, or MVB—the version of a team that can move, learn and create the most value the fastest and with the least effort. The lean startup soared in popularity throughout the twenty-tens, but it's almost impossible to practice lean startup without a lean bureaucracy.

An MVB has just enough processes to support operations without sacrificing the speed and employee morale required to innovate and stay competitive. At its core, an MVB demands that you have a precise reason for each individual process requirement.

Building upon the work of Adam Rose from technology firm Dialexa, I've developed the following simple framework to help organisations move towards becoming a minimum viable bureaucracy:

MVB = Value ↑ / Bureaucracy ↓

Ultimately, you'll want to increase the value your organisation creates, while decreasing the bureaucracy, or steps required, to create that value—without compromising the quality of output to an unacceptable level.

If you're a one-man band, you can apply this formula to your own work to gauge where you're at.

The following non-exhaustible lists of levers can help you increase value while decreasing bureaucracy. (I'll deep dive into many of these levers in part 4.)

To increase value:

- stretch your product S-curve (cross-sell, up-sell, explore new customer segments and geographies)
- share learnings with other parts of the business and replicate wins
- leverage customer referrals
- increase marketing spend on higher performing products
- focus on objectively high-value activities.

To decrease bureaucracy:

- automate rudimentary and process-oriented tasks
- outsource what can't be automated to talent-on-demand
- decrease the number of people required to make Type 2 decisions
- lower delegations of authority so decentralised command can reign and bottlenecks decrease
- eliminate or mitigate silos so bottlenecks decrease and collaboration becomes more fluid
- focus on building the proverbial 'four-button remote control', which does the job, instead of the 100-button remote control, which is far surplus to requirements
- work with external partners to complement and speed up your efforts
- decrease the frequency of effort or action (e.g. frequency of reporting or meetings)
- use data to inform decision making instead of professional judgement alone
- stop doing things that aren't adding much, if any, value.

Speed is fundamental to innovation

For so many of today's typical organisations, speed is not their strongest hand—in fact, it's usually their 2-7. Speed is why small, relatively cash-strapped but nimble startups are able to out-perform and disrupt large incumbents, because they aren't weighed down by bureaucracy and process.

When it comes to speed, organisations such as Spotify find themselves holding a royal flush (see figure 8.2).

Some things that jump out are:

- *trust* > control
- agile at scale requires *trust* at scale
- small cross-functional tribes
- *alignment*.

As we can see, there can be no MVB without trust. That's why getting the right people on the bus is key to making this work.

Transparency

According to a report by Interaction Associates on building workplace trust, people trust each other on the job based on one of the following reasons:

- consistency, predictability and quality of people's work and actions
- confidence that they are focused on achieving shared goals
- expectations associated with a person's role in the organisation.

Earning trust requires the development of a culture that practices consistency, predictability and transparency.

We don't trust our barista when the quality of our morning cup of coffee differs from day to day. If it's too hot one day, and too cold the next, they will see us taking our business elsewhere. This is especially true if you find yourself in a coffee hotbed like Melbourne where there are numerous hip and high-quality cafés on each city block.

We don't trust people who say one thing to our faces, but do another behind our backs.

By the same token, we don't trust unpredictable colleagues, because we don't know which version of them is going to show up — the version that gets the proverbial coffee hot, cold or just right.

A lack of transparency and predictability brings down trust faster than a bratty 10 year old gleefully eyeing off a painstakingly put-together house of cards.

Radical transparency

Hedge fund manager and founder of Bridgewater Associates Ray Dalio popularised the notion of radical transparency in his bestselling book, *Principles*.

Radical transparency is a belief that organisations should be open, honest and straightforward, rather than keep the discussion of certain details behind closed doors. It's about not sugarcoating what we really think of each other's performance, to help address problems and move the organisation forward.

Dalio created a culture where employees candidly share feedback and ideas without drawing criticism from others. This shortens their feedback loop, and establishes an environment where there are no elephants in the room, an environment where people *trust* each other.

Bridgewater has also developed a proprietary application called Dots.

The app facilitates the rating of fellow employees across more than 100 attributes such as creativity, common sense and dealing with ambiguity. They use this to praise or critique colleagues.

Social media company Buffer shares its sales numbers, salaries and revenue allocation publicly. Henceforth, the world watches.

Other companies take radical transparency and extend it to their customers.

Wearable tech company FitBit is transparent about which user data points it collects, how it shares them and how the collection of adult data differs from the collection of children's data.

Patagonia is transparent about where all of their products come from, how they were made, where raw materials were sourced and what textile worker conditions are like. From a commercial perspective, this reinforces the quality of Patagonia's products. It contributes to customers being more willing to spend top dollar on their products, not just because of the quality, but because of the moral stance that Patagonia has taken.

Of course, building trust gets easier if you have the right people on the bus to begin with.

Get the right people on the bus

If there isn't values alignment between the company and its people, it's akin to two people of equal strength trying to jumpstart a vehicle, but with one pushing from the rear and the other from the front. As a consequence, either the car stays idle or someone gets run over.

When you have values alignment, you successfully jumpstart the vehicle and proceed to have one hell of a road trip.

Rather than trying to fit square pegs into round holes and change people after the fact, ensuring alignment *before* hiring people renders the battle mostly won before it's begun.

How? Well, for starters you should:

- ensure your organisation's culture and values are clearly understood and defined
- define what kind of personal character attributes people who fit this culture possess.

When you go to market, ensure there is alignment between A and B.

The best people aren't always looking for a job, because they're in high demand, so you should leverage your network first and search on LinkedIn to target suitable candidates before advertising a role.

You might attract top talent to your organisation through your existing employees, who serve as brand ambassadors, providing you've built an awesome culture.

You might create compelling content and initiatives that paint your company in a positive light.

When my company ran the Mills Oakley legal-tech startup accelerator program, the law firm reported a higher number of quality candidates applying to work for them afterwards. This was because candidates associated the firm with being more innovative and progressive by virtue of the accelerator program.

During interviews, don't just ask candidates *what* they did previously, but *why* and *how*. This will tell you more about the way they think, how much they contributed to outcomes and whether said outcomes were the result of positive behaviours or dumb luck.

Find out what *process* they followed to get to said outcome. Never conflate an outcome with the quality of a decision alone because there are many variables that impact outcomes, and many of them are out of our control. You can have a good outcome underpinned by bad behaviours, and a bad outcome underpinned by good behaviours, but over the long term, good behaviours will come out on top.

Tease out from your questions, not only information about a candidate's past experience and hard skillset, but, more importantly, how they have demonstrated sought-after 21st-century character attributes such as resilience, problem solving, creativity, economic literacy and adaptability, among others: 'Tell me about a time when you persisted, even though it would have been much easier to give up.'

Inspire them with talk about the company's vision and what they can expect to achieve and realise at your organisation.

What if you can't afford to get the best people on the bus?

I posed this question to Netflix co-founder Marc Randolph on the *Future Squared* podcast. Marc was instrumental in getting people to join Netflix during the early days for half of what they'd make elsewhere, before they even had a viable business model.

The answer?

'Give them something to believe in.'

The best people aren't driven just by dollars. The best people are emotionally intelligent enough to know that above a certain point, more money won't bring them more happiness, and that what they desire more is meaningful work with meaningful people. If your company is working on a worthwhile mission and you can find people whose values are aligned with this mission, then what it takes is crafting a compelling story about where your company is going.

As Bezos did at Amazon, and Musk did at Tesla, it's about selling the future, not just the present. And when you do that effectively, getting the best people to hop aboard becomes a lot more plausible than trying to merely lure them your way with dollars and cents.

RESULTING

Former World Series of Poker champion, Annie Duke, calls our tendency to conflate outcomes with decisions, 'resulting'. She tells the story of Pete Carroll, coach of the Seattle Seahawks, in her book *Thinking in Bets*. With just 26 seconds left on the clock in Superbowl XLIX, the Seahawks were on the New England Patriots' one-yard line. They could smell victory and had the Superbowl trophy in their grip. Carroll told his quarterback to pass the ball, instead of run it over the line. The ball was intercepted and the Seahawks lost.

While the media was quick to crucify him, Duke notes that based on 15 years of NFL data, the probability of a short-pass being intercepted was just 2 per cent. And if a pass is incomplete, the

---

clock stops automatically, giving the offence another chance at glory.

When you analyse the facts, it was bad luck more than a bad call on Carroll's behalf.

It turns out that 'it's not whether you win or lose, it's how you play the game' is more than just a throwaway line to make kids feel better about losing.

Iron sharpens iron

If you want to hire top tech talent, you need to demonstrate that you have such talent, or a vision to build a top team. If you already have top tech talent, bring them along to interviews with tech candidates (high performers are attracted to high performer cultures and people).

As Netflix co-founder Marc Randolph wrote in his book *That Will Never Work*, most engineers can choose where they want to work, and where they decide to work boils down to two questions:

1. Do I respect the people I'm working for?
2. Will I be given interesting problems to solve?

Incentivisation

Incentivise accordingly.

Use both extrinsic motivators (cash and tangible rewards) and intrinsic motivators (growth, autonomy and purpose). Most organisations won't be able to pay at the top of market like Netflix do, but intrinsic levers are in reach of most companies.

Having said this, avoid mercenaries who *only do things for the pay*.

Per Machiavelli's advice to Florentine prince, Lorenzo de Medici,

Mercenary and auxiliary forces are useless and dangerous; and any ruler who keeps his state dependent upon mercenaries will never have real peace or security, for they are disorganized, undisciplined, ambitious, and faithless... The reason for all this is that they have no tie of devotion, no motive for taking the field except their meager pay, and this is not enough to make them willing to die for [a prince].

High performers are curious about the world around them.

Take a moment to review a candidate's social media profiles to find out whether they demonstrate a curious mind. If you're hiring for a role that requires curiosity, and a candidate's social media profile is littered with links to television's *The Bachelor* and not much else, then they're *probably* not all that curious about the world and are merely consuming whatever is served up on a silver platter via mainstream media outlets. On the other hand, if they're sharing and following all kinds of esoteric and obscure things, while not conclusive in itself, it's more likely that they're a curious cat.

Doing all of this will help you avoid, or at least minimise, what political scientists and economists call the principal-agent problem, which occurs when one person (the employee) is allowed to make decisions on behalf of an entity (the company). This presents conflict of interest, which is manifest by uninspired employees the world over watching the clock and trying to get away with doing as little work as possible. This is why getting the right people on the bus and incentivising accordingly is critical.

When you have conflicts of interest between principals and agents, you end up with the likes of Theranos and WeWork, clear cases of self-interested founders compromising—and in the latter case, sacrificing—the potential of their organisation and their people, as well as an abundance of investor dollars.

Keep them on the bus

First, ensure they are set to perform. Establish measurable performance indicators from day one so they know where they stand. There should be no surprises if someone isn't performing. If they aren't, take corrective action early. Don't let it linger as it will only exacerbate the problem for them, for you and for the organisation. Have open, transparent and regular conversations from day one, not just once or twice a year.

Give new hires everything they need to succeed (when people don't perform, it can often be a result of their environment rather than their character).

Say thank you. Acknowledge people for their efforts, and ensure they feel appreciated and part of the team. Simple advice, but sometimes Occam's razor holds true.

Finally, create an environment where people have a sense of autonomy — an opportunity to constantly learn and challenge themselves and align with the mission of the organisation.

This includes creating an environment and culture where people can rise to the level of their capabilities instead of fall to the level of the organisation's rituals and environment. We'll explore this further in the next chapter.

CALL TO ACTION

Build a time-rich culture with the following action items.

1. Reflect on the MVB formula. How can you decrease B while increasing V?

2. Start practising radical transparency — it won't be easy at first, but once you see the benefits, you'll start to appreciate the discomfort.

3. Do you have the right people on the bus? If not, how can you get them and keep them on the bus?

4. If you've got a team, reflect on your incentives, or lack thereof, and ensure that both intrinsic and extrinsic motivations are tailored to.

5. To help you get buy-in from people who can influence company culture, download our free ebook on the topic at bit.ly/22waystogetbuyin

CHAPTER 9
Toxic work culture and environment

The modern workplace is characterised by unnecessary meetings and counter productive expectations of hyper-responsiveness. This has only been further heightened by the new wave of open-plan offices, which is leaving people more prone to interruption than ever.

In this chapter, I introduce why these are toxic and present a number of easy-to-implement tools and techniques to loosen their grip and reap immediate benefits in your workplace.

Meetings: the good, the bad and the ugly

According to research from scheduling tool Doodle, which studied 19 million meetings and interviewed over 6500 professionals, pointless meetings cost US companies alone US$399 billion in 2019. That's more than the GDP of countries like Singapore, the United Arab Emirates, Hong Kong and Sweden.

I lost count of the number of multi-hour meetings (with 10 or more people present) I attended while working for top-tier consulting firms. In most cases, only two or three people were required, and the desired outcomes could have been reached in 30 minutes or less, instead of two hours. This was one of the galvanising reasons behind my quitting to pursue entrepreneurship.

A 10-person, two-hour meeting is a 20-hour meeting in terms of the cost to the organisation. When you consider hourly billing rates, the true cost of these to an organisation can be well upwards of $5000, if not $10000, depending on who is present—and that doesn't even account for opportunity cost.

These meetings aren't necessary evils, they're stupid.

At Collective Campus:

- We don't have meetings for the sake of meetings.
- Our initial sales prospecting and exploration calls are 15 minutes by default.
- Only the people who need to be at the meeting are present instead of the cast of thousands you'll find at a traditional firm.
- We use Slack to share little tidbits asynchronously, instead of meeting.
- Nobody can block time in somebody else's calendar; you need to ask first and get a buy-in that a meeting is warranted.
- We ensure that there is a specific agenda and focus on it.
- We avoid trivial small talk and walk out of the meeting with action points, responsible persons and due dates.
- We don't meet to transfer information. Information transfer can be done far more efficiently, and when it suits the recipient, via IM or email.

Here's our meeting checklist.

MEETING CHECKLIST

» Only hold a meeting if it is absolutely necessary and the same outcomes can't be reached via a quick ad-hoc conversation, phone call, email, text or instant message.

» Set the meeting to 15 minutes by default, and only make it longer if absolutely necessary (the shorter the meeting, the more succinct you will have to be, and the less time there will be for pointless small talk and rambling).

» Set a specific agenda and desired outcome going into the meeting.

» Invite only 'must have' people (unless this is a big Type-1 decision, two people should usually do it with three on the rare occasion).

» Opt to have the meeting standing or walking, so that people don't get too comfortable, are more alert and want to wrap it up.

» Ban devices from being used in the meeting, unless relevant to the meeting.

» Agree on next steps, allocate responsible person(s) and set due dates (this is especially important to avoid boomerang meetings).

As Jason Fried — co-founder of Basecamp — puts it, companies spend their employees' time and attention as if there were an infinite supply of both, and as if they cost nothing, but they are the scarcest resources we have.

Basecamp practises 'protectionism'. You can't just block out time in a colleague's calendar — hell, you can't even see their calendar. Instead, you need to *sell a meeting to a colleague*. Only if they can see the value in the meeting do they tell you when they're available and for how long.

Given what we learned earlier around early birds and night owls, you might want to block out certain parts of your day for deep work. While people can see my calendar, they can only schedule times that I have made available for meetings. These meeting windows are usually between 1 and 4 pm on Tuesday through Thursday. That way, I'm free in the morning — when I'm at my best — to focus on high-level cognition work, while I tend to have meeting-free days every Monday and Friday.

Invite only relevant people who can add value or ensure things move along once the meeting has concluded. There's usually little point inviting or being a third wheel at a meeting, unless your organisation has trust and ownership issues.

Travel

If I need to travel 30 minutes each way for a 30-minute meeting, that's not a 30-minute meeting—that's a 90-minute meeting.

If I'm catching a flight from Melbourne to Sydney for a 60-minute meeting, that's not a 60 minute meeting, but about an eight-hour meeting when you account for flight and transit time.

When you fly in a pressurised cabin, you also become dehydrated and lose fluids more quickly. According to Dr Diana Kerwin, chief of Geriatrics at Texas Health Dallas, this is why we feel like crap after a flight. Flying eats away at our ability to perform at a biological level.

In today's hyperconnected world, most meetings can be attended remotely via videocall.

As AngelList founder Naval Ravikant puts it, 'Meetings should really be phone calls, phone calls should be emails, and emails should just be texts. You have to, just drop non-urgent meetings or forget them altogether if you want to do anything great.'

Ravikant has actually given up travelling for business altogether.

I tend to shy away from business travel unless it's mission-critical, it can't be resolved remotely, it's a key client delivery, or it will be fun and add to my quality of life. Nowadays, if I'm going to travel for business and it just so happens to be to a coastal city, I'll arrange for the appointments to take place at the start or at the end of the week, I'll stay near the beach and spend the weekend exploring and surfing. Whenever possible, integrate work and play.

Asynchronous communication

'I'll get to it when it suits me.' This is the nature of asynchronous communication.

The reality is that most things don't require an immediate response. For most things, a one-way email or instant message should do the job, with the recipient responding when it suits them.

If something really is urgent, then the mode of communication should reflect that. Pick up the phone, or tap that person on the shoulder, but only if it is truly urgent. If it's not urgent, you're merely disrespecting their work, and you risk feeding a culture of constant interruption, one that's devoid of flow.

Tools

The following tools enable the steering of an asynchronous ship:

- email
- instant messaging to support non-instant responses (Slack, Facebook Workplace, Microsoft Teams, WhatsApp)
- project management tools (e.g. Asana, Trello, Basecamp and JIRA) enable you to ask questions, assign work and check in on progress, all without having to interrupt anyone
- periodic standup meetings (batch your need-to-know team communication with standup meetings but try to keep these short and the frequency functional) — can also be performed via instant messaging)
- intranet (Yammer, SharePoint)
- inbox pause and Block Site (block inbound communication for set periods of the day).

Aside from the massive benefit of giving people more time for uninterrupted focus, asynchronous communication predisposes people to making better decisions than they would with synchronous communication. As Robert Greene says, if you want to cut emotion out of the equation, increase your response time. Giving people time to think between question and response, rather than fall victim to blurting out the first thing that comes to mind, delivers a compound benefit to the organisation. It's about being proactive rather than reactive.

In order to avoid tennis games and duplication of effort, ensure that asynchronous messages:

- provide sufficient background detail, where necessary
- provide clear action item(s) and outcome(s) required

- provide a due date
- provide a path of recourse if the recipient is unable to meet your requirements.

For example:

Hey Shay

Attached is the incorporation document for our new spin-off company.

Please sign the document where requested and send it back to me by 4 pm this Friday.

If you have any concerns, give me a call on 555 1983.

As with email, in an asynchronous company, batch-checking IM platforms becomes key, in order to avoid spending all day chasing red dots and sharing all manner of gifs with your colleagues.

Speaking of which, platforms like Slack will 'strongly recommend' that you turn on desktop notifications. Don't. This satisfies their platform engagement KPIs while sacrificing your own focus and productivity.

THE EISENHOWER PRINCIPLE

Understanding the difference between urgent and important goes a long way in this regard, which brings me to the Eisenhower Principle.

US President Dwight D Eisenhower famously said, 'I have two kinds of problems, the urgent and the important. What is important is seldom urgent, and what is urgent is seldom important.'

So what did he actually mean by urgent and important?

» *Importance:* how valuable something is; subjective professional judgement. One man's trash is another man's treasure.

» *Urgency:* how soon something needs to be done. This is more of an objective judgement; what is due tomorrow is more urgent than what is due in a week.

Before you start tackling urgent tasks only, most deadlines are arbitrary dates set by people who don't have to do the work themselves. Most urgent tasks aren't actually urgent. See the Eisenhower Matrix in figure 9.1.

	Urgent	**Not urgent**
Important	**Q1** Urgent *and* important	**Q2** Important *and* not urgent
Not important	**Q3** Urgent *and* not important	**Q4** Not important *and* not urgent

Figure 9.1: the Eisenhower Matrix

You'll note that only urgent *and* important tasks should be done right now. Bear this in mind before prioritising 'inbox zero' above all else, or interrupting your colleague for that relatively inconsequential piece of work that's not due for 30 days.

Many emails fall into the Q4 bucket, yet we spend a good chunk of our days responding to these emails instead of deferring, delegating or deleting them.

Similarly, you must establish boundaries with clients and colleagues when it comes to your availability and responsiveness.

The folly of open-plan offices

The move towards open-plan offices was supposed to make offices more collaborative and productive.

But as Sue Shellenbarger wrote in an article called 'Why You Can't Concentrate at Work' for *The Wall Street Journal*, they've had the opposite effect. 'All of this social engineering (open-plan offices) has created endless distractions that draw employees' eyes away from their own screens. Visual noise, the activity or movement around the edges of an employee's field of vision, can erode concentration and disrupt analytical thinking or creativity.'

Sabine Kastner, a professor of neuroscience and psychology at Princeton University, has for over 20 years, studied how the brain pays attention. She says that for some people, an open-plan office can make it almost *impossible* to concentrate.

Not only that, but in most organisations, people tend to default to sitting in proximity to familiar people. 'Chance collaboration', a touted benefit of open-plan offices, is not much different from the water cooler conversations that have been a hallmark of corporate offices since day one.

In truth, the 'collaboration' argument was a front for cost-cutting, with the average square footing per employee shrinking by 33 per cent in just seven years. When you apply that number to big, hairy and expensive commercial real estate leases across hundreds or thousands of staff, we're talking about lots of savings.

And as Shellenbarger pointed out, professionals are being interrupted more than ever.

The following stats provide for some pause.

- 71 per cent of people are frequently interrupted at work.
- 28 per cent of employee time is spent tackling unnecessary interruptions, which is followed by recovery time (more than two hours of a typical employee's workday).
- The average employee is interrupted 50 to 60 times a day (approximately once every eight minutes).

- We suffer an IQ dip of 10 points when we're fielding constant emails, texts and taps on the shoulder—this is on par with pulling an all-nighter.
- Interruptions cost the US economy US$1 trillion a year (Jonathan Spira, author of *Overload!*).

SHORTER HOURS DOES NOT MEAN LESS PAY

Much of the criticism of my *Harvard Business Review* article, 'The Case for the 6-Hour Workday', has come from people who conflate shorter hours with less pay. But nowhere do I indicate or suggest that this has to be the case. On the contrary, if done well, it means paying people more by virtue of better outcomes.

It *may* mean, however, in a trust-based organisation that prioritises commitment over consensus, scales back on meetings and unnecessary red-tape, that there will be nowhere to hide. In a perfectly Darwinian organisation, as opposed to a collectivist Marxist one, this means that only the best people are left standing.

As Reed Hastings of Netflix says, when you hire slow and fire fast, you increase the organisation's 'talent density' over time.

Those left standing reap the rewards of a higher performing organisation with a smaller pool of employees—a larger pie is shared among fewer people.

Somewhat controversially, embracing concepts like minimum viable bureaucracies, outsourcing and algorithm-driven business models means that your organisation will find it difficult to redeploy all of its talent. This is effectively the law of natural selection in play, and echoes what former tech adviser to Barack Obama, Alec Ross, says: there will be no room to be mediocre in the future.

You'll find a 'How to run a shorter workday' experiment guide in the appendix.

(continued)

SHORTER HOURS DOES NOT MEAN LESS PAY (*cont'd*)

Price's law and why you should fire most of your team

British physicist and historian Derek Price is best remembered for an observation he made, now known as Price's law.

The law states that the square root of the number of people in a domain create 50 per cent of the value, as shown in figure 9.2. This means that in a company of 100 employees, 10 create half the value, and in a company of 1000, just 31 create a staggering 50 per cent of the value!

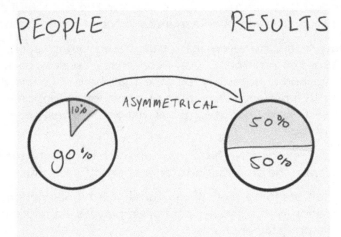

Figure 9.2: Price's law
Source: Darius Foroux (www.dariusforoux.com/prices-law)

Unlike the famous Pareto Principle, Price looked at this concept purely from the perspective of work and value creation.

Nowhere to hide

The smaller the organisation, the more obvious it will be just who is doing half of the work, and the less room there will be to hide.

Conversely, the larger the organisation, the more room there will be for passengers to strap in and enjoy the ride.

As legendary physicist Richard Feynman said, to make reality out of abstract, use an example.

Let's take the 2019 NBA championship-winning Toronto Raptors.

Of the 22 players on its roster, the top four players (the square root is 4.7), led by Kawhi Leonard, scored 53 per cent of the team's 3460 regular season field goals.

You might observe this phenomenon in your own organisation, particularly in your sales department, where the top five salespeople in a team of 25 may well generate half the business.

Price and politics

Price's law also explains why, in large organisations, you'll find lots of people looking to prove themselves. Unfortunately, it's not through the quality of their work, but through aligning themselves with the right people, and playing politics and charades.

As Netflix co-founder Marc Randolph wrote in his book, *That Will Never Work*, 'In many disciplines, being a smooth talker or snappy dresser can grease your assent to the executive suite but in Silicon Valley, the only thing that really matters is the quality of your work.'

The more confident someone is in their abilities, the more likely they are to challenge the status quo, because they're okay with getting fired, confident in their abilities to get hired and thrive elsewhere.

Hire slow, fire fast

Fortunately for the passengers hitching a ride out there, it is not only easier to hide in a large organisation, but it's also much harder to get fired. This is because large companies have more to lose, and the regulator's spotlight is often shining in their general direction.

Rather than raise the ire of regulators, risk unfair dismissal lawsuits, become the object of negative media attention and face a dwindling stock price, it's far easier to keep paying under-performers and have the square root of their people cover their losses.

Getting fired from a large company usually isn't a matter of a trigger-happy boss sending a fax your way *Back to the Future* style; it usually requires a long, drawn-out period of warnings and counselling before someone can be safely let go.

(continued)

SHORTER HOURS DOES NOT MEAN LESS PAY (*cont'd*)

Contrast this with the 'hire slow, fire fast' mantra that embodies many small companies and startups.

Build a lean machine

During the early days of Netflix—pre-IPO—external circumstances meant that the company needed to let go of a large number of its people. As Marc Randolph noted, 'Winnowing our staff made us lean and more focused. With superstar players doing all of the work, it was no wonder that our quality of work was very high.'

This echoes what great writers such as Stephen King say about writing: 'Kill your darlings'. Great writers know that it's usually a matter of writing more than you need to, and then cutting and re-writing most of what you write. Rather than work your way up to 50 000 words, writing 100 000 and then picking only the best bits is likely to produce a more polished book.

From a business perspective, being left only with the best talent also means that it becomes easier to *attract* talent. Again, Randolph reminds us that 'it's much easier to attract other elite talent to your team when you've established a reputation for superstar talent'.

Reflect on your team and its results, who is contributing most of the value and who is coasting.

You might need to make some hard, but very valuable decisions.

As Sweden's minister for employment, Ylva Johansson, said, 'The jobs disappear, and then we train people for new jobs. We won't protect jobs. But we will protect workers.' Organisations might face similar responsibilities as governments when it comes to protecting long-serving workers that they ultimately part ways with. Keeping jobs for the sake of people having jobs does them, the company and the economy no favours in the long term. What does is keeping people employable to do valuable work that a machine can't do.

Not only that though. Once a person's skillset no longer aligns with the opportunities available at that organisation, it's not only in the organisation's interests that they move on, but as we've already established, also in their own.

Pay by the hour

Only for professions that are paid by the hour does the question of 'What about pay?' become relevant. Putting aside the obvious conflicts of interest that hourly billing presents, there are numerous things you can do in this space to mitigate those conflicts and incentivise performance in line with this book's principles — for example, sufficient bonuses or incentive payments for finishing a project by a certain date; or paying out a fixed percentage of a remaining contract value if the job is finished early, increasing the effective hourly rate.

If a project is set to take me 100 hours to complete at a $50 hourly rate, it's worth $5000 to me. But if I finish in 50 hours and get paid 50 per cent of the remaining contract value as a bonus, I get $3750, but my effective hourly rate is $75 (50 per cent higher) and I've liberated 50 hours (worth $2500) to work on other projects, or to live.

Consider this arrangement if you're an employer or a contractor.

The obvious caveat here is that so long as the contractor can find ongoing work to keep them as busy as they want to be, everybody wins. When the gig market is weak, it's in a contractor's interests to extract as much monetary value out of an engagement as possible.

Next, it's time to explore what we as individuals do that sabotages our potential.

CALL TO ACTION

Practise better work with the following action items.

1. Stop travelling locally or further abroad if a phone call or video call will suffice (be vigilant!).

2. Prioritise your common tasks into the Eisenhower Matrix and schedule in time for important but not urgent tasks.

3. Create an environment for several hours a day where you won't be interrupted.

4. Run a 'shorter workday experiment' in your team (check out the appendix).

CHAPTER 10
How individuals kill productivity

'4'. The number stared back at me. It took a moment to process.

Four hours a day.

I did some quick maths in my head.

This was the equivalent of eight weeks a year, or about 16 per cent of the year, or nearly one-quarter of my waking hours!

What was I referring to?

The amount of time I spent staring at my smartphone.

What was I doing on my smartphone?

Bouncing between email and social media.

Was any of this work remotely necessary? No.

Was it rewarding? Far from it.

If anything, it served as a distraction that kept me from confronting just how bored I was and from pursuing more rewarding endeavours.

Today, it's easy to use social media as a surrogate for genuine human connection.

But social media and texting are no substitute for genuine human connection. As Cal Newport wrote in his book, *Digital Minimalism*, human beings have evolved to build strong social connections with family, close friends, and community through face-to-face interactions that require non-trivial sacrifices of time and energy.

But for longer than I'd care to admit, that's where I was.

'I haven't got a problem with technology; I can stop using it if I want to!'

I didn't want to be a zombie, mindlessly scrolling through my smartphone.

Buoyed on by the digital minimalist movement, I decided that I would make my phone my slave, rather than submit to it as my master. I'd use it intentionally, simply to make plans with friends and occasionally share useful content with them, rather than conversate ad infinitum. I call it digital *essentialism*, rather than minimalism.

So what *is essential*?

As my daily screentime slowly decreased, I realised that I was short on genuine human connection, and I wasn't living life as much as I should be. I wasn't fully living up to a question I often like to ask myself: 'Will I remember this in five years?'

If my days are full of things I won't remember in five days, let alone five years, then I'll find myself on my deathbed, full of regret.

As decorated US journalist, author (and night owl) Hunter S Thompson said, 'Life should not be a journey to the grave with the intention of arriving safely in a pretty and well preserved body, but rather to skid in broadside in a cloud of smoke, thoroughly used up, totally worn out, and loudly proclaiming "Wow! What a Ride!"'

With that in mind, I set off to make some drastic changes.

The now obvious hole in my evenings forced me to get out more, to schedule more activities with my girlfriend, to schedule more dinners and nights out with friends and to see more standup comics perform.

It forced me to hit the open-mic standup comedy circuit myself. I started attending networking events on topics of interest where I could connect both with likeminded and, maybe more importantly, *different*-minded people. More connection and deep conversations, less small-talk about the weather.

Would I remember these things in five years? Hell yeah.

SMALL TALK DOESN'T MAKE YOU HAPPY

A 2018 study at the University of Arizona found that small talk is essentially an inactive ingredient insofar as our mental wellbeing is concerned.

The research team gave 486 students devices that would record intermittently throughout the day.

A recording every 12.5 minutes for 30 seconds gave them a total of 23 689 files.

Conversations were grouped into small talk—trivial interactions about the weather—and then deep conversations—such as life philosophies, identity politics or relationships.

Research leader and psychology professor Matthias Mehl told *Business Insider* that 'people who reported being more satisfied with their life spend less time alone and more time surrounded by other people'. He went on to say that they also have more substantive conversations.

According to Mehl, small talk was an inactive ingredient, producing neither positive nor negative outcomes.

Tools are only as good as *how* you use them. Our collective relationship with technology and social media is having a devastating effect on our personal productivity and emotional wellbeing.

As in any 12-step program, step one is admitting you have a problem.

But it's not just technology. There are numerous ways we consciously and not so consciously sabotage our best work, day after day.

Inbox zero: the badge of (dis)honour

Research by Adobe found that employees spend an average of six hours per day on email. Another study found that the average employee checks email 74 times a day. This means we're checking email once every six minutes. It takes us 23 minutes to get back into flow after switching tasks, so the average person's email habit ensures that they are spending *no* time in flow at all.

Cleaning out our inboxes lulls us into a false sense of control and productivity. Being really good at getting to inbox zero, a badge of honour in most workplaces, means that you're great at putting other people's priorities ahead of your own.

In the past five years, I've accumulated over 71000 unread emails (see figure 10.1)—and that's just my business inbox. I've received 107000 emails, and sent just 40000 (many of which were automated).

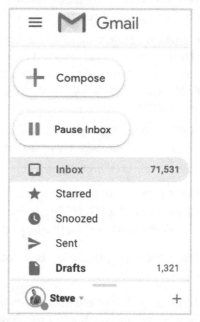

Figure 10.1: my inbox
Source: Google and the Google logo are registered trademarks of Google LLC, used with permission.

This comes back to urgent versus important. Either you respond or you defer, delegate, delete or in my case, do not reply. What ills has not responding to those 71 531 emails caused? The past five years have been the most rewarding of my life. I credit *not* being glued to my inbox as one of the reasons for it.

The obsessive-compulsive among you might be freaking out, but it comes back to focusing on what matters to you, not someone else.

I tend to batch check and respond to important emails two to three times a day, while others, like Jonathan Levi from SuperHuman Academy, only check email twice a *week*. If you put into place good systems and set expectations, you can get away with reducing how often you check email.

CHECKING EMAIL STRESSES US OUT

Batch checking email is not only beneficial for your productivity, but also for your stress levels and emotional health. A study from the University of British Columbia found that when people checked email just three times a day, their stress levels decreased *significantly*.

They found that when study participants limited checking email to just three times a day, they experienced significantly lower stress than those who could check email unlimited times a day.

The researchers wrote that 'lower stress predicted higher well-being on a diverse range of well-being outcomes. These findings highlight the benefits of checking email less frequently for reducing psychological stress'. There's something to be said, however, about the nature of emails in your inbox.

Pro tip: Deleting email apps from your phone makes a world of difference. Once I did that, I never looked back.

Not sure how much time you're spending hanging out in your inbox? Check out RescueTime, a tool for your desktop that tracks just how much time you're spending on various applications. It's not just the time you spend *in* email, but the effect on your work of task-switching to check email. Getting back in the zone isn't as simple as switching tabs on your MacBook.

Task-switching vs multitasking

Newsflash: Multitasking is a myth.

It's actually task-switching. We can't actually pay attention to and work on two things at once.

As we've established, once an interruption, or an internal trigger, has forced us to switch between tasks, it can take us about 23 minutes to get back to the task at hand.

'But I'm just checking email. It only takes a second.'

Recent estimates find that even if a task-switch wastes only one-tenth of a second (glancing at a push notification on your phone) it can add up to a 40 per cent productivity loss if you do lots of switching over the course of a day. This number might be higher if benchmarked against a high-productivity executive or founder.

Instant gratification

Human beings are programmed to take the path of least effort, according to a study out of University College, London. Researchers found that our brains trick us into thinking that the nearest beach has the best waves. We have a cognitive bias moving us away from the effortful decision.

Tim Urban, curator of the incredibly popular Wait But Why blog, sees the rational decision-maker in your brain as unwittingly coexisting with a pet he dubs the 'Instant Gratification Monkey'.

'[The monkey] thinks only about the present...and he concerns himself entirely with maximizing the ease and pleasure of the current moment...Why would we ever use a computer for work when the internet is sitting right there waiting to be played with?'

This is evolutionary programming. And it made sense when it came to evading predators on the African savannah and having sufficient energy to catch elusive prey after a several-day fast. It was all about survival.

Nowadays, these intuitions sabotage us more than they serve us. We're no longer fighting for survival on the African savannah. We have access to more food than we can handle. (Too much food if you consider the alarming upswing in the percentage of Americans diagnosed with diabetes over the past 60 years.) Not to say anything of obesity rates, or the total daily calories we tend to consume, which has more than *doubled* in Europe since 1700.

Nowadays, in order to prosper, we need to intercept our evolutionary programming.

Mindfulness students will be familiar with the acronym STOP.

Stop

Take a breath

Observe

Proceed

We should apply similar steps when it comes to catching, and intercepting our evolutionary programming, as it usually compels us to do the easiest thing at the expense of our longer term goals.

Want to be successful? Avoid instant gratification.

It's tempting to start our days by checking social media or reading company mentions online, responding to emails, reformatting PowerPoint documents or attending 'educational' breakfasts. All of these tasks are easy and don't require us to apply much, if any, critical thinking. They're *easy*.

Doing the hardest things first

Whether we start our workday at 8 am or 8 pm, we should focus on doing the hardest things first. We should almost exclusively focus on the hard and valuable things because, as we'll learn in chapter 11, the other things should either be automated, delegated, outsourced or simply not done at all.

But it can be easier said than done to sit down and get started.

Staring at a blank canvas can be confronting for the most seasoned artist. But it's just a matter of doing the smallest possible piece of work to build momentum.

You might also want to engineer environmental cues into your day to trigger certain types of activities. For example, my mental association with sitting down at my local café, in a seat facing the street, with my laptop in front of me, is that it's time to write. Whereas if I was to try to write in my bedroom (something that should only be associated with two things, one being sleep), I'll struggle to get going anywhere near as fast.

It may feel like we're going against the laws of physics when we start on a task that requires mental focus — and in some ways, we are.

ISAAC NEWTON'S LAWS OF MOTION

According to Isaac Newton's first law, an object at rest stays at rest, and an object in motion stays in motion. The tendency of an object to remain at rest is known as inertia. Mass is a good measure of inertia; light objects are easy to move, but heavy objects are much harder to move. Objects at rest will only move when they encounter an unbalanced force.

So, what's an unbalanced force?

Say there's a block atop a table. There are two forces acting upon the block: the downwards pull of gravity and the upwards push of the table — these forces 'balance' each other out, so the block stays still, as illustrated in figure 10.2.

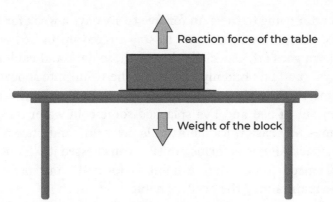

Reaction force of the table

Weight of the block

Figure 10.2: balanced forces acting on a block

Now, say someone slides the block from right to left, and there is nobody pushing the block from the left side. This is an unbalanced force, and so the block moves.

When we're struggling to get started with a difficult task, it's because the push of our will is weaker or equal to the force of our evolutionary programming, forcing us not to do anything. They operate in lockstep like unbalanced forces, and so we keep procrastinating.

If heavy objects are much harder to move, you will need to dig deep, and it may feel like you're deploying the crane or the wrecking ball of your mind just to get started. But if you deploy that wrecking ball every day, over time the object will become comparatively small, to the point where you won't need a proverbial wrecking ball, but maybe just a light kick with your Chuck Taylors to get going. This is the essence of habit formation.

Speaking of habit formation, James Clear, author of *Atomic Habits*, suggests we can build transformational habits simply by focusing on the smallest possible unit of effort. If you're looking to develop into a regular gym goer, Clear doesn't suggest setting yourself a target of working out for 60 minutes a day from the get-go. Rather, he suggests setting yourself a target of going to the gym regularly for just *five minutes*. After a week or two of turning up for five minutes a day, you'll start to tell yourself, 'Well, I'm here every day, I may as well train for a little longer.'

Even after going to the gym for five to six days a week for the past 14 years, part of me still wants to stay rugged up in bed when my 6 am alarm goes off, especially during those dark and colder winter mornings — and I do find myself hitting the 10-minute snooze button from time to time for a little beauty sleep. But without fail, every time I'm out of bed and I've splashed some cold water on my face, it becomes way easier. Momentum is powerful, and once a habit is formed, it actually stays formed until — you guessed it — it encounters an unbalanced force. After a habit is formed, your default state becomes maintaining the positive habit.

You might find the same when you sit down to read. Sometimes, you might instead prefer to vegetate on the couch. But if you've willed yourself to pick up a book, you'll find it considerably easier to turn to a second page than it was to pick the book up in the first place.

Tim Ferriss' daily writing quota is just 'two crappy pages a day'. Those two pages help him get started. It's not about the quality — it's about getting started. Writing a 1000-word article from scratch may seem like a Herculean task, but once you've got 100 words down — no matter how crappy — you get into your groove.

The cost of doing nothing is usually a lot more than doing something poorly at first, and gradually improving it.

When it comes to overwriting biological programming, simply set yourself a small but achievable target that prevents you from being overwhelmed by the entire task, and you'll find that once you've reached that target, it will be much easier to continue than to stop. This is partly because you'd be basking in an accomplishment-driven hit of dopamine, which helps us see rewards and move towards them. This is also why short feedback loops are more important in a business setting than five-year plans.

Handy hack

When I asked author Ben Mezrich how he gets into his groove when he first sits down to write, his advice was short and solid. 'I stop writing in the middle of a sentence. That way, when I sit down to write, I just finish that sentence, and I'm writing.'

Whatever hard task it is that you're working on, find a way to stop in the middle so that when you sit down (or stand up) to continue tomorrow, you simply pick up from where you left off, making it much easier to get into the rhythm of things.

Some like to put on their gym gear before they go to bed, so that when they get up in the morning they're already dressed and ready to go!

Residual work

Most people have a tendency to spend time on a specific task long after most of the value has been delivered — like reformatting that PowerPoint presentation for the seventeenth time!

I witnessed this first-hand countless times at large consulting firms, where six-figure-earning MBA graduates would 'painstakingly' spend their time moving an object in a proposal document millimetres to the left, and then to the right, and then to the left, before replacing the object altogether and repeating the cycle.

In all of these cases, the revenue-generating value had already been delivered, but a desire to 'perfect', as well as optimise, their efforts for the easiest and least mentally taxing activity, results in the graduate wasting hours of time.

The difference between high performers and everybody else is that high performers know exactly when they need to stop. They are super tuned in to the point of diminishing returns (see figure 10.3, overleaf).

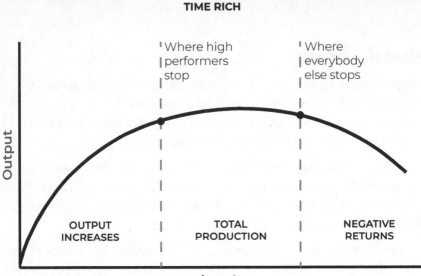

Figure 10.3: point of diminishing returns

This bell curve beautifully demonstrates the tendency of most people — buoyed on by evolutionary programming, perfectionism and insecurity — to keep working long after *enough* value has been created.

Knowing what 'enough' is, is not only a powerful tool when it comes to productivity, but also when it comes to how you live your life. It's not uncommon for people to work themselves silly to attain more, when they already had enough to live a contented life, true to themselves, long ago.

Push notifications

As I wrote for *Harvard Business Review*, the sight and sound of smartphone and desktop rings and dings characterises the typical workplace, and it's keeping competent executives in a state of Pavlovian hyper-responsiveness.

'But what if I miss something important? It only takes a second to check.'

We now know that this is faulty reasoning given the impact of micro-switches on productivity, and the endless rabbit holes that email and social media present us with.

A slot machine in our pockets

Nir Eyal, author of *Hooked* and *Indistractable*, established that tech companies are essentially leveraging a vulnerability in human psychology to keep us hooked. Whether it be an internal trigger (for example, for a desire for social connection) or an external trigger (for example, a push notification), the hooked cycle begins. We promptly respond to such triggers by taking an action (for example, open Instagram), bask in the dopaminergic reward ('Oh look, someone liked my photo!') and make further investments into the platform (for example, respond to the like). The hooked cycle rolls on, but the next internal trigger might be 'I wonder if they responded yet?' Rinse and repeat.

Google's former design ethicist and founder of the Center for Humane Technology, Tristan Harris, says carrying a smartphone is like having a slot machine in our pockets. We can't resist but take a spin every few minutes.

Salesforce founder and CEO Marc Benioff has been vocal about his concerns, suggesting that Facebook should be regulated like cigarettes. However, it's not just Facebook; most successful tech companies are employing similar strategies.

By occupying ourselves with a steady stream of small, non-consequential 'accomplishments' that make us feel good in the moment, we stay busy but end up moving no closer to our goals.

Like any tools, it comes down to how you use them.

In the knowledge worker age, having the time and ability to disconnect and have original thoughts is the true scarce and valuable resource.

Save your best for the playoffs

The Stoic philosophers of Ancient Rome were proponents of living in accordance with nature.

One may take 'nature' to mean many things, and the Stoics have not been without their critics on this point, including Friedrich Nietzsche.

To borrow from Marcus Aurelius's *Meditations*, 'Don't you see the plants, the birds, the ants and spiders and bees going about their individual tasks, putting the world in order, as best they can? And you're not willing to do your job as a human being? Why aren't you running to do what your nature demands?'

So, let's take 'nature' to mean what we observe in the natural world — nature's examples, be they of ecology, fauna, flora or the wider cosmos.

Earth has not one, but four seasons, each serving a purpose.

Animals too have seasons. Bears hibernate through winter to escape the cold and inevitable food scarcity. Many birds fly south to temperate climates during the winter, and to nesting grounds in the north during summer.

Perhaps a perfect example of living in accordance with nature can be found not on National Geographic, but on ESPN: professional sports. No team sports league runs around the clock, 52 weeks a year. They have seasons: offseason, preseason, regular season, playoffs and finals. The NBA's offseason runs for a good four months — six if your team failed to make the playoffs (something I'm used to, being a Phoenix Suns fan).

The intensity that NBA players are expected to work at during the 82-game regular season versus the seven-game finals series is radically different.

Yet, when it comes to the modern workplace, especially that of many a corporate and startup office space, we tend to behave as if it's Game 7 of the NBA Finals *all year round* (except for the silly season, of course). There *will* be times when you have to dig deep, when you have to burn the midnight oil. But you can only do that for so long without suffering a serious degradation in performance overall.

Like a hunter-gatherer on the African savannah who hasn't eaten for days, success, and survival, depends on knowing when to conserve energy, when to tread lightly and when to pounce with all you've got.

★ ★ ★

When we say we're time poor, what this often means is that we're decision poor. By now, it should be clear that how we choose to allocate our time is the problem. We say 'yes' to too many things, we spend too much time in our inboxes, we prioritise the important over the urgent...the list goes on.

In part 4, we will dive into how you can become time rich by improving the quality of your decisions, and expose you to a wide range of actionable tools and techniques, many of which you can start to apply to your work today.

CALL TO ACTION

1. Have more meaningful conversations and use weather or small talk as a trigger to change tack.

2. Stop treating inbox zero like a badge of honour and instead try to batch check and respond just one to three times a day.

3. Turn off all push notifications (google 'How to turn off push notifications') and put your phone on Airplane mode when concentrating deeply on work.

4. Focus on one task at a time (stop task-switching!).

5. Stop working on a task long after most of the value has been delivered (know what 'good enough' is).

6. Do the hardest thing first, and suppress your desire to do instantly gratifying but unrewarding things.

7. Introduce a 'continue here' equivalent to your work.

8. Reflect on what your offseason, regular season, playoffs and finals are, and act accordingly.

PART 4
HOW TO BECOME TIME RICH

So far, we've looked at the origins of the eight-hour workday, the evolution of work and how both organisations *and* individuals sabotage their potential.

The tools and techniques presented in part 4 should help you level up your decision making, which has the capacity to make your team and your organisation several times more productive without the need to work longer hours, and can give you a lot more freedom to reinvest into other dimensions of life.

Given that we evolved to use our core senses long before we started using language, I've created a visual mnemonic — PeaCOATS — to help you remember the building blocks to freedom and reaching your potential.

PeaCOATS is a helpful way to remember the building blocks of becoming time rich. It stands for:

Prioritise, **e**conomies of scale and **a**lignment

Cut waste

Outsource (and delegate)

Automate

Test and iterate

Start your engine.

There's one thing to note (for those of you who are sure to pick up on this): while the acronym is PeaCOATS, you'll find that A comes before O in the following chapters. This is because you should always automate things that can be automated before thinking about outsourcing them as the latter incurs a higher cumulative cost and is subject to human error, whereas if something can be automated, the long-term cost is low, and notwithstanding tech issues, a lot more reliable.

CHAPTER 11
Pea: Prioritise, economies of scale and alignment

To-do lists are helpful productivity aids, but what happens when your to-do list runs over an entire page and leaves you feeling overwhelmed, with little control of your work? We've all been there before.

I announced my team's '6-Hour Workday' experiment on LinkedIn. A connection responded almost immediately, 'It's nice in theory, but I can't finish all of my tasks in six hours!' As if all tasks were created equal.

The law of nature that is the Pareto Principle stipulates that about 20 per cent of your tasks will create about 80 per cent of the value. So it's time to prioritise.

I strive to ensure that what's on my to-do list has been subject to some kind of deliberate prioritisation.

This helps me see the trees from the forest, maintain my composure and focus on the activities that are going to truly move the needle and bring me closer to my objectives.

Additionally, focusing on tasks that are aligned with my — and my business's — strengths, and where I can tap into economies of scale, augment the value of every hour I invest.

Productivity is what you don't do

This goes deeper than just tasks to what you *do*. Period.

The foundations of productivity and effectiveness are underpinned by why you do the work you do in the first place, and what it is you actually do.

As famed management thinker Peter Drucker purportedly said, 'Productivity is what you don't do.'

THE GOLDEN CIRCLE

Simon Sinek put forward his idea of the 'Golden Circle' in his bestselling book, *Start with Why*. The idea was that you identify your purpose first (your 'why'), your process second (your 'how') and your 'what' last.

When tackling the question 'Why?', you must first ask what *your* why is right now.

It's easy to get sucked into the matrix. It's easy to grind out work, day after day. It's easy to look around at our colleagues, all similarly immersed, and conclude that, 'Well, this must be the way it's supposed to be.'

Mark Twain famously said, 'Whenever you find yourself on the side of the majority, it is time to pause and reflect.'

So many people resign themselves to a false belief that work isn't supposed to be something they enjoy. They never take the time to reflect on what would make them happy and fulfilled in their work, or whether those two words can usefully be paired to begin with.

I'd like to borrow from the Golden Circle, but flip the 'what' and 'how', insofar as productivity is concerned.

To be your very best, you'll need all three to operate in lockstep.

Why: doing something that aligns with your purpose or values, something that you truly believe in

What: doing something that you are naturally good at, and enjoy, and something that helps you deliver on your *why*

How: doing your *what* in the most effective way

My why: to unlock the latent potential of people to create more impact in the world and lead more fulfilling lives

My what: education and advisory work (workshops, books, podcasts, blogs, EdTech, investing, consulting)

My how: by prioritising, outsourcing and automating the stuff that's rudimentary, repeatable or that I suck at, I can focus on what I'm best at and what I enjoy most: creating content.

If you have a powerful *why*, but your what isn't the best way to go about it, then the how doesn't matter. If you have a powerful *why* and *what*, but you're spending your days in pointless meetings and checking emails the rest of the time, your productivity and endgame will pay the price.

Jim Collins' Hedgehog Concept takes this concept further by incorporating monetary reward. Essentially, he proposes that you do something you're deeply passionate about, something you can be the best in the world at, and something that drives your economic engine.

A word on *what* you do

As Albert Einstein is believed to have said, 'Everybody is a genius. But if you judge a fish by its ability to climb a tree, it will live its whole life believing that it is stupid.'

Economies of scale

In pure microeconomic speak, economies of scale are cost advantages associated with the larger scale of operation; costs per unit decrease with increasing scale.

By leveraging advantages you might have as you, or your organisation, grows, you can effectively do more with less. Whether that be through productising what you do, through the automation of tasks, by repurposing and re-using content (which we get to later) but also by leveraging domain expertise, assets, customers, networks and partners you've worked hard to develop for other things.

For example, it was much easier for UBER to roll-out UBER Eats than it was UBER proper because the technology infrastructure, driver network and customer database already existed.

Alignment

At our core, everything we do at Collective Campus is about unlocking the latent potential of people at organisations to create impact and lead more fulfilling lives. That includes large companies, SMEs, startups, individuals and children. There is alignment.

Joe Rogan knows a thing or two about excelling at many things, but also about alignment.

Rogan hosts *The Joe Rogan Experience* podcast, he's a UFC commentator, an internationally acclaimed comedian, co-founder of nutrition company Onnit, former Taekwondo champion, Brazilian Jiujitsu black belt and former TV presenter.

At first glance, it seems like he's got a lot of disparate things going on. Upon closer inspection, you'll find alignment between his years honing his communication as a comedian and his podcasting, TV presenting and UFC commentating. His BJJ and martial arts background, in general, helps him leverage his communication skills as the UFC's go-to commentator.

Before you do anything suggested in this chapter, gaining alignment across your why and what will go a long way to helping you become way more productive, and an actualised version of yourself.

The Pareto Principle

Italian economist Vilfredo Pareto noted the 80/20 connection while at the University of Lausanne in 1896, and published his findings in his first work, *Cours d'Économie Politique*. Pareto showed that approximately 80 per cent of the land in Italy was owned by 20 per cent of the population. But this phenomenon doesn't stop there.

Did you know that:

- about 80 per cent of the cars on our roads occupy about 20 per cent of the roads?
- 20 per cent of the words in the English language occupy about 80 per cent of the pages in our books?
- 20 per cent of an organisation's customers contribute to about 80 per cent of the revenues?
- 20 per cent of software bugs are attributable to about 80 per cent of the issues?
- 20 per cent of the Fortune 500 accounts for about 80 per cent of the total market cap of the index?

This universal law of nature shows up everywhere.

If you apply 80/20 to 80/20 (that is, 80% × 80 and 20% × 20), you soon find that the law can be broken down to 64/4, 50/1 or even 40/0.2.

That means that 4 per cent of an organisation's customers could be responsible for 64 per cent of its revenue.

In a world of noise, knowing how to find the proverbial signal — and prioritise the 4 per cent — is the difference between reaching the summit and being stuck at sea-level.

What Super Mario and Vilfredo Pareto have in common

I decided to test this theory and find the signal in the noise of the video game market, inspired by a podcast conversation with Blake Harris, author of *Console Wars: Sega, Nintendo, and the Battle that Defined a Generation*.

Mobile games

Nowadays, walk onto any form of public transport and you'll be hard-pressed not to find people of almost any demographic playing mobile games. The convergence of cloud, mobile and social has resulted in a 10-times increase in the number of gamers in the world, which today stands at more than 2.3 billion.

It's not hard to find examples of the Pareto Principle at work when it comes to mobile gaming.

Adweek found that 70 per cent of in-app purchase revenue comes from just 10 per cent of in-app purchasers (also known as 'whales'), accounting for *59 per cent of total revenue.*

Sony PlayStation

The top 30 Sony PlayStation games of all time sold a combined 115 million units.

The top 20 per cent of these sold 66 million units (60 per cent), topped by *Uncharted 4* (15 million units sold), *Marvel's Spider-Man* (13.2 million) and *The Last of Us* (10 million).

Xbox 360

The top 63 Xbox 360 games of all time sold a combined 225 million units.

The top 20 per cent of these sold 131 million units (59 per cent), topped by *Kinect Adventures!* (24 million units sold), *Grant Theft Auto V* (17.79 million) and *Halo 3* (14.5 million).

Nintendo Entertainment System

Nintendo is an old childhood favourite of mine.

The top 75 NES games of all time sold a combined 236 million units.

Of these, the top 20 per cent sold 141 million units (again, 60 per cent). Again, about 60 per cent of sales.

Unsurprisingly, the list was topped by *Super Mario Bros.*, which alone accounted for almost 20 per cent of the top 75's sales (40.24 million units sold), followed by *Duck Hunt* (28.3 million units), *Super Mario Bros. 3* (18 million) and *Super Mario Bros. 2* (7.46 million).

The results here are more 60/20 than 80/20, maybe because we're ignoring the long tail-end of also-rans and bombs. What's striking though, is that in all of these cases, the top 20 per cent of these consoles' bestselling games account for the majority of sales.

To check out other examples and dive into the data, read my extended post at www.steveglaveski.com/blog/super-mario-and-the-80-20-principle.

Lessons learned

What this tells us is that, whatever your focus — video games, sales channels, marketing strategies, customer segments, product features, employee hires and so on — the universe will almost mandate that the top 20 per cent will deliver the lion's share of the value (or on the flipside, the lion's share of the pain, as is the case with difficult customers or employees, who you may be well advised to let go).

In order to get the absolute most out of your time and money, and improve your performance many times over, identify and amplify your 20 per cent: don't build a 100-button remote control when a four-button remote will do.

80/20 WEBSITE OPTIMISATION

I could spend 100 hours optimising 100 pages on my company website to increase conversion rates. But if I apply the Pareto Principle, one page should get 50 per cent of the traffic. If I spend just one hour optimising my website, then I'll get half the value I would spend optimising 100 simply by tweaking this one page.

Let's test this theory!

For the period 1 March to 31 May 2019, our blog received about 10 000 unique page views. (By December 2019, about 20 000 unique users were visiting our site each month.)

The top 100 pages received 8446 unique page views. Here are the blog rankings:

Rank	Page	Unique page views
1	/blog/10-companies-that-were-too-slow-to-respond-to-change	1798
2	/ (home page)	1386
3	/blog/future-squared-episode-203-perry-marshall-on-80-20-sales-and-marketing-2	829

The top page received 1798 page views.

Not quite 50 per cent, but 21 per cent.

The top three pages scored 4013 unique page views, or 48 per cent of the top 100. As such, we should prioritise the optimisation of these pages, instead of on all 100 pages. We should ensure that calls to action (e.g. email sign-up forms) are more apparent and compelling on these pages, and that we invest more time and money distributing these popular pieces of content online. Perhaps we can use these signals to inform subsequent webinar, workshop or keynote talk topics.

This is how you save heaps of time and create heaps of value — by focusing on the signal, *not* the noise.

Perry Marshall put forward the case of gate attendance at professional sports stadiums to illustrate this point in his book *80/20 Sales and Marketing*. While you might get 20 000 people to pay $20 each for a ticket, pocketing $400 000 in the process, there will also be 1000 or so people collectively paying for and/or occupying 200 corporate boxes. At $5000 a pop, they bring in $1 million: these are your high-value customers. In this case, high-value customers represent 5 per cent of the total audience but generate 72 per cent of the revenue.

Once you know what to work on, you still may find yourself with a list of several things to do on any given day. So how do you prioritise your 'to-do' list?

Instead of an overly complex model that nobody would use, I've been using the following model (see 'How to prioritise your tasks') for a number of years. It helps me make sense of my day and priorities. Give it a try.

How to prioritise your tasks

Now that we appreciate the why of prioritisation, it's time to dive into the how.

A simple prioritisation chart like table 11.1 should help you to see the proverbial trees. You can augment this by using it in conjunction with a Kanban board, a visual representation of your tasks as they make their way from 'to-do' to 'doing' and 'done' (see figure 11.1, overleaf). Tools like Trello or Asana are helpful aids, as are good old-fashioned sticky notes.

Table 11.1: how to prioritise tasks

Task	Value	Cost	Urgency	Result	Prioritise
Admin	5	3	0.3	0.5	3
Report	7	7	0.5	0.5	3
Reply	7	2	0.8	2.8	1
Talk	6	8	0.7	0.525	2
Research	7	8	0.4	0.35	4

Start by creating a backlog of tasks, as per the example in table 11.1.

Step 1: Give each task a rating out of 10 in terms of the value you think it will deliver.

Step 2: Give it a rating out of 10 for cost (time and money—the higher the cost, the higher the rating).

Step 3: Divide value by cost.

Step 4: Apply a weighting to the urgency of step 3.

Step 5: Prioritise by the final result and move this task into the 'Doing' column on your Kanban board while leaving the rest in your 'To-Do' column (see figure 11.1).

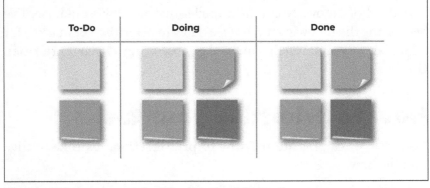

Figure 11.1: an example of a Kanban board

You can use tools such as Trello, Asana, Evernote or even Excel or Sheets to manage your own personal Kanban.

So, now that you've prioritised your tasks, it's time to do what George Foreman once urged, and cut the fat.

CALL TO ACTION

1. Are you doing work that aligns with your strengths, natural inclinations, interests and purpose? If not, identify what changes you can make—big or small—that can bring you closer to alignment.

2. What economies of scale can you or your team tap into?

3. Reflect on and identify your 'signal in the noise' tasks, clients, marketing channels and so on.

4. Prioritise your tasks using the value/cost method and capture it on a Kanban board (be it physical or online).

CHAPTER 12
C: Cut the fat

In their book *How to Think about Weird Things*, Theodore Schick and Lewis Vaughn wrote, 'The quality of your life is determined by the quality of your decisions, and the quality of your decisions is determined by the quality of your thinking.'

The same applies in business.

When it comes to making decisions, you have to cut the waste. You have several options:

- Outsource the decision where possible.
- Automate the decision if reliably repeatable.
- Make the decision now (if important).
- Delay the decision until later (if less important).
- Do nothing.

Should you choose to make the decision, you need to avoid various pitfalls: poor data, cognitive biases, inadequate experience and politics, to name a few.

When it comes to team decision making, groupthink and the most dominant and highest paid person's opinion also factor into the equation and can seriously derail the quality of our decisions.

What use is having a good mix of 'the right people on the bus' if we aren't leveraging them to make decisions? After all, decisions are what determine where our organisations — and we — end up.

The Rule of Two

Silicon Valley coach Bill Campbell was a proponent of the Rule of Two to make better decisions. He would get the two people most closely involved in a decision to gather more information and work together on the best solution. They usually came back having decided together on the best course of action. This might sound counterproductive insofar as how efficiency-minded MBAs see the world.

While the first order of consequence is using two resources instead of one to make a decision, the second is a *better decision* and outcome. The third is a more effective working relationship between the two parties. It really comes down to what you're optimising for — what outcome are you looking to achieve?

I shouldn't have to tell you by now that the Rule of Two should not be applied to Type-2 decisions, which people should be making themselves.

Another Rule of Two is arm wrestling. Ken Kutaragi built Sony's now dominant video-game business, but he wasn't so domineering when it came to arm wrestling then-Sony executive Bernie Stolar, to decide whether or not to manufacture a larger version of the Sony PlayStation controller for the US market, something Kutaragi had opposed. In retrospect, it turned out being the wrong decision, seeing as Sony eventually scaled back the size of the US controller to the original version.

Of course, I'm only joking about resorting to arm wrestling to make strategic decisions — but hey, if it's a stalemate ...

Organisational debt

Organisational debt is what Behance founder Scott Belsky calls one of the biggest productivity killers. It's essentially the accumulation of decisions that should have been made but weren't, adding unnecessary weight to the organisation.

If you make the wrong decision, you learn faster than by forever agonising over what the right decision is.

Belsky suggests making decisions quickly, so long as your organisation is tuned to reverse the wrong decision quickly. It clears cobwebs, keeps people engaged and clears organisational debt.

How to make team decisions

I've been using the following framework with my team for several years whenever we make important Type-1 decisions.

Rather than risk groupthink, anchoring or the most vocal person's opinion rising to the top, we take a leaf out of the world of agile management and design thinking, and 'work alone together'.

We assemble a team of meritable people (usually three and no more than five) who are credible when it comes to the subject matter.

We'll individually take the time to rate options across criteria we've determined (see figure 12.1) and then share our ratings with the group.

Any significant discrepancies (more than one, for example, 8 vs 6) will be discussed. A team member might have a greater appreciation for the subtle nuances around a particular area—for example the technology, economics or regulatory landscape. They are given an opportunity to explain their rating. After explaining, the group is more informed, and a new round of voting commences until there is no more than one discrepancy across the board.

This approach means that we use data plus cross-functional professional judgement to mitigate the impact of cognitive biases and our own mental baggage. It mitigates the risk of the data leading us astray. You should always strive to be data-informed, not data-driven.

Option	Variable 1		Avg	Variable 2		Avg	Variable 3		Avg	Subtotal	Weight	Total
A	9	8	8.3	7	8	7	7.3	6	5	6	5.66	21.26	1.2	25.51
B	7	6	7	6.6	6	5	6	5.6	6	6	6	6	17.6	1.1	19.36
C	5	6	5	5.3	5	5	5	5	8	7	8	8.3	18.6	1.3	24.18

Figure 12.1: how to make team decisions

To summarise working alone together:

- *Step 1:* Decide which decisions to make.
- *Step 2:* Make a list.
- *Step 3:* Establish a decision criteria (for example, price, quality, speed, service etc.).
- *Step 4:* Rate and discuss.
- *Step 5:* Rinse and repeat.

ICE

A simple decision-making alternative is the ICE model, which stands for Impact, Confidence and Ease. Participants rate options across the criteria shown in figure 12.2 out of 10 (10 being best, 1 being worst), add results to get to the ICE score and prioritise by the highest ICE score. In the example in figure 12.2, the upsell campaign would be prioritised.

Idea	Hypothesis	Impact	Confidence	Ease	ICE
Referral program	Customers love us enough to refer their friends	9	7	6	22
Upsell campaign	Customers need additional support	9	8	6	23
Reddit campaign	Raising awareness via Reddit will increase traffic	7	3	4	14

Figure 12.2: an ICE prioritisation matrix

Mental models

While we can find mental models for decision making in the works of Aristotle, Plato and Seneca, mental models have (almost) gone mainstream. We're living in an age when academics such as Jordan Peterson routinely sell out 5000 theatre seats at $100 a pop. People, in particular millennials, are *hungry for knowledge,* and they're buoyed on by the lower barriers to entry and endless possibilities that the internet presents them with.

This has spawned the success of communities such as Shane Parrish's Farnam Street blog (featured in a *New York Times* article in late 2018); the success of independent media outlets such as *The Joe Rogan Experience* podcast and *The Tim Ferriss Show* podcast; and books such as Ray Dalio's *Principles,* among others.

A mental model is a representation of how things work. We evolved to neatly categorise things, for better or worse, into neatly demarcated buckets so we can make sense of the world. Mental models navigate complex situations and help us make better decisions.

Parrish suggests that the quality of our thinking is proportional to the mental models in our heads. For example, if we know that delaying gratification usually renders more positive outcomes, then we are more likely to try to delay.

As Charlie Munger, Warren Buffett's partner in crime, posited,

the first rule is that you can't really know anything if you just remember isolated facts and try and bang 'em back. ...You've got to have models in your head ...students who just try to remember and pound back what is remembered ...fail in school and in life.

Let's look at some mental models that will help you make better decisions and cut the waste.

First principles thinking

Entrepreneurs such as Elon Musk, Jeff Bezos and Peter Thiel credit their success to first principles thinking—what Musk calls a

physics way of looking at the world ...you boil things down to the most fundamental truths and say, ... 'what are we sure is true?' ...and then reason up from there.

John Boyd, decorated US military strategist, put forward the following thought experiment.

Imagine you have three things:

1. a motorboat with a skier behind it
2. a military tank
3. a bicycle.

Break these parts down into their constituents:

1. motorboat: motor, hull, skis
2. tank: metal treads, steel armour plates, gun
3. bicycle: handlebars, wheels, gears, seat.

Now re-assemble the constituent parts to create something new.

Boyd proposed a snowmobile, combining the handlebars, seat, metal treads, motor and skis.

This is the essence of first principles thinking: deconstruct then reconstruct.

It might sound easy but as human beings, we tend to optimise for form rather than function. We also tend to anchor on what we already know and only incrementally improve that.

Consider this: while Ancient Roman soldiers had wheeled chariots, it wasn't until 1970 that the first rolling suitcase was invented by Bernard Shaw. Up until that point, luggage, and oftentimes heavy luggage, was carried by hand.

Second order thinking

Shit happens when we think about things only from the perspective of first order of consequence. 'If I rob this bank, then I will have lots of money' might sound great until the second order consequence kicks in: that of spending the next 10 years in prison.

Playing out not only the second but third, fourth and fifth orders of consequences of our decisions is a hallmark of the critical thinker. Considering only the first order consequence is akin to kids failing the famed marshmallow test because they can't hold out from eating a solitary marshmallow for 15 minutes.

Counterfactuals

When considering the merits or otherwise of how things have turned out, be it in the political, business or personal domains, consider the counterfactual; that is, what if events had transpired counter to the facts — the alternatives.

For example, many on the left side of the political spectrum have been up in arms since Donald Trump was elected President of the United States in 2016. What about the counterfactual, though? As Ed Kilgore writes for *New York Magazine*, 'there would be no Democratic resistance...there's no reason to think Democrats would not have remained relatively united. Who knows what Donald Trump would have done in defeat?'

He says that it's always useful to reflect on what might have been and what might not have been all that different from our reality.

Hanlon's razor

Hanlon's razor suggests that we should not attribute to malice that which is more readily explained by stupidity. Or as Seneca said, 'People do wrong through ignorance, not intent.' This one has helped me to navigate some otherwise treacherous relationships, see the good in everyone and adjust my behaviour accordingly.

The inverted U

In life, we grow up thinking that the more of a good thing we get, the better. More money, more education, more friends. But too much of a good thing is not only too much, but can actually be bad for us, and can have debilitating consequences.

In his book *The Paradox of Choice*, psychologist Barry Schwartz asserts that while having no choices tends to be undesirable, having too many choices can render us paralysed by options and never fully committing to a decision because we wonder whether we could have done better. This shows up in various aspects of life. Whether it's deciding what to eat at a Japanese restaurant, choosing which job offer to take, determining a place of abode, which product to buy or which romantic partner to settle down with.

Schwartz puts forward the case that there are two types of people in the world. No, not people who divide the world into two types of people and people who don't. I'm talking about satisficers and maximisers.

Satisficers tend to settle for the good-enough option while maximisers look for the best possible option. Schwartz says that maximisers tend to make better decisions more often, but they are generally unhappier than satisficers. This is because their decisions are usually laced with regret and the 'grass is greener' complex. Compare this with the satisficer, who fully commits to a decision once it has been made, resulting in a more content and happier existence.

Schwartz captured this notion beautifully as illustrated by the inverted-U curve in figure 12.3.

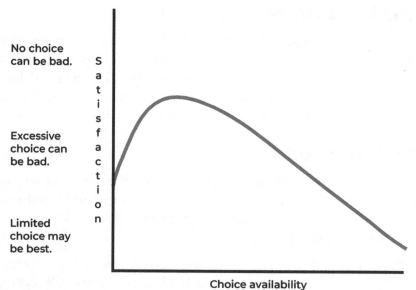

Figure 12.3: choice paradox and satisfaction
Source: Adapted from *The Paradox of Choice* by Barry Schwartz

The reality is that anything taken to extreme can harm us, even things that on the surface seem nothing but good for us — exercise, planning, kale salads, technology consumption, networking, work, sleep, regulation, processes, content consumption, travel, money and even stress, all of which in just the right dose can spur us into action and get us into flow, but too much can be debilitating.

For a list of 109 mental models, check out https://fs.blog/mental-models.

The challenge then becomes not what mental models are at your disposal, but when to use them.

The way things have always been done

'That's the way we've always done things around here.'

As Socrates said, the unexamined life is not worth living; so too the unexamined work life. If you're doing things 'just because', but haven't reflected on why you're doing them, take a moment to do just that.

My first real business endeavour was a web startup called Hotdesk, essentially an Airbnb for an office space type marketplace. I spent so much time doing the easy stuff, like writing emails to my mailing list of several hundred people. I spent nowhere near enough doing the hard stuff, like trying to find product-market fit. Two years after inception, I shut down the business; it had over 1300 locations listed, but nowhere near the amount of demand required to make the business cash-flow positive and sustainable.

Perhaps if I had taken time to reflect on what I was doing that wasn't adding value, I would have had more time to spend on the things that did.

As an aside, I had no genuine interest in being a glorified real estate agent, and Hotdesk failing opened the door to subsequent business pursuits, which were way more rewarding, as well as writing books like this one. Out of darkness comes light, and that light is a manifestation of alignment with strength, purpose and what you enjoy.

The strategy quadrant

Peter Drucker is believed to have said that 'there's nothing worse than the wrong things done right'.

On a quarterly basis, my team reflects on a strategy quadrant (see figure 12.4, overleaf) and spends an hour talking through which of our tasks, clients, marketing strategies, sales strategies, geographies, features, products and so on we should start, stop, do more of and do less of.

For every one thing we add, we need to remove something, so that we don't end up being spread too thin across too many things, and being mediocre or poor at all of them.

This is something you can apply to your personal workload, as well as your personal life more broadly, so that you spend your time on things that deliver value.

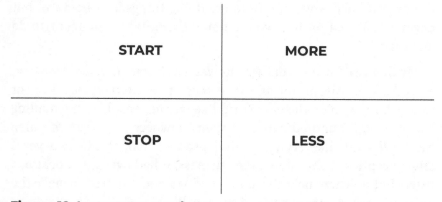

Figure 12.4: strategy quadrant

Why you should say 'no' to almost everything (and when to say 'yes')

Beware of the sage on the stage.

I attended a business networking event while writing this book.

I had the misfortune of witnessing a 'sage on the stage' (a random local entrepreneur with modest levels of success, likely earned through timing, sheer persistence and luck as opposed to deliberate practice) who spewed forth the following verbal diarrhoea.

Say 'yes' to everything.

He proceeded to trace his own personal journey and said that saying 'yes' to things is what had put him on a collision course with opportunity-creating serendipity.

How to call bullsh*t

Whenever someone uses personal anecdotes, you should be wary because they are likely falling victim to the narrative fallacy — our tendency to condense complex events into easy-to-understand narratives, and essentially draw a linear story (we learned about this in chapter 6). As anybody who has had some level of success knows, success is anything but linear — and as Behance founder Scott Belsky said on the *Future Squared* podcast, 'We tend to misattribute our success to things we'd rather remember than things we'd rather forget.'

Such anecdotal advice is also flawed for the following reasons:

- A sample size of one obviously isn't sufficient, as any scientist will tell you.
- It is easy to disregard all of the times you said 'yes' that didn't create any meaningful opportunity, or forget the times when saying 'no' did.
- Most things aren't black and white.

And perhaps the most poignant ...

- Every time you say 'yes' to something, you're saying 'no' to everything else.

Saying 'no' is fundamental to our ability to navigate the world around us. Can you imagine a world in which you responded to every advertisement you saw, entertained every cold caller, responded to every random email from an offshore web developer or search engine optimisation (SEO) consultant, attended every Facebook event, allocated capital into every investment opportunity you were presented with and attended every meeting with someone who reached out to 'pick your brain'?

You would find yourself out of time and out of money, very, very quickly.

Not only that, but you would be putting other people's priorities ahead of your own.

How to say 'yes' or 'no' consciously

In order to best evaluate opportunities and say 'yes' or 'no' consciously, you must first define your north star:

- Who do you want to be (your values)?
- Where do you want to go (your objectives)?
- How will you get there (the process)?

When I took my first entrepreneurial steps back in 2012, I wanted two things: to live a life true to myself (values) — away from the bullsh*t politics of the corporate world — and to build a business where I could earn at least what I was making in the corporate world (objectives).

In terms of process, I initially frequented meetup events that brought like-minded people together to talk shop. But I quickly realised that I could learn whatever I needed far quicker through podcasts and books (process), and that the overwhelming majority of people I met weren't people I could learn anything worthwhile or immediately applicable from.

So I stopped going to such events and instead invested heavily into consuming targeted material that would help me overcome any business challenges I was having — because it's unlikely that the 100 people at networking events are all facing the exact same challenge at the exact same time.

This was a far better use of my time and got me closer to my north star — much faster than drinking cheap beer and eating pizza, and making small talk with 'wantrapreneurs' at startup meetups could ever have done.

What about serendipity?

Serendipity is a thing, and chance encounters can create significant opportunities or meaningful relationships, but these encounters are few and far between. For every person I've met at a networking event who created some kind of opportunity, I've met hundreds more where I wish I could have got that time back.

As such, while you should say 'no' to almost everything that doesn't align with your north star, it makes sense to create space for an oxymoron I like to call 'deliberate serendipity'.

This essentially means saying 'yes' to things you'd normally say 'no' to — but only on occasion. The frequency with which you say 'yes' should become apparent to you the more you practise.

Saying 'no' is a competitive advantage

In a world where people shy away from conflict and fall victim to the path of least resistance, the ability to disconnect, say 'no' and focus is a massive competitive advantage.

It gives you more of that commodity that, once spent, you will never get back: time. As Ancient Roman philosopher Seneca put it, 'It is not that we have so little time but that we lose so much...life we receive is not short but we make it so; we are not ill provided but use what we have wastefully.'

CALL TO ACTION

1. Reflect on your 20 per cent tasks, clients, marketing channels and so on.

2. Test out the decision-making activity with your team.

3. What can you cut?

4. Apply the strategy quadrant to your business and life.

5. Define your 'north star' and use it to better evaluate opportunities, invites and requests.

CHAPTER 13

A: Automation

In a world driven by algorithms, if you're not automating, you're probably being left behind. Nowadays, all kinds of business tasks can be automated—some you probably thought were beyond the domain of computers.

Sadly, too few entrepreneurs and business executives are taking advantage of the multitude of cheap and easy-to-use tools on the market. Too often they end up manually performing repetitive tasks themselves and go on to complain (or brag?) that they're so busy all the time and can't keep up with their workload.

Table 13.1 presents just some of the tasks you can automate across a business's value chain.

Table 13.1: a snapshot of what you can automate

Department	Example tasks
Legal	Data mining, contract review
Sales	Lead generation, lead nurturing, proposal development, meeting preparation, customer intelligence, competitor intelligence
Marketing	Email templates and marketing, content syndication, content repurposing, content distribution
IT	Data backups, network management, PC maintenance, account creation, file transfers, data extraction, testing

(continued)

Table 13.1: a snapshot of what you can automate (*cont'd*)

Department	Example tasks
HR	Payroll scheduling, candidate recruiting
Development/ programming	Scripts to copy files and perform repetitive actions, the optimisation of images
Customer support	Surveys and questionnaires, customer enquiries

Sales and marketing automation

Let's deep dive into some of the tools you can leverage across the value chain. Given the fast-moving nature of the world, new tools worth using are being released often, so I'll be keeping a living, breathing list of tools to help you optimise your game at timerichbook.com/tools. Subscribe for regular updates.

Sales tools

One way to scale your sales efforts is to hire a huge team of sales reps — but that can be costly, and finding capable people can be challenging.

Nowadays, you can scale and optimise your sales efforts using technology, at a fraction of the cost of relying on human beings alone. Whether it's prospecting, proposals or closing, automation tools can help you level up your game big time across every step in the sales cycle.

App	Find out more at	Features and benefits
Lead prospecting and nurturing		
Conversica	conversica.com	• a customised, online persona that automatically contacts, engages, nurtures, qualifies and follows up on leads via natural, two-way email conversations until the lead converts into an opportunity • notifies actual sales reps immediately resulting in a much higher likelihood of closing the lead

MixMax Snov.io SendGrid	mixmax.com snov.io sendgrid.com	• help you find, validate and send personalised email drip-feeds to target customers
		• enable you to build in rules to send subsequent emails based on whether or not a recipient opens or responds to a first or second email
		• empower your team to send hundreds, if not thousands of targeted, personalised prospecting emails a week
		• SendGrid offers an even more sophisticated suite of offerings in this space, including marketing automation, design and templates
GMass	gmass.co	• enables you to schedule emails, send out mass emails, mail merge campaigns and more directly from Gmail
Alfred	meetalfred.com	• a LinkedIn social selling automation tool to automagically view LinkedIn profiles, send connection requests and personalised messages, monitor your and your team's performance and send unlimited follow-up messages at pre-determined intervals

Other prospecting tools that are worth checking out include Prospect.io, LeadIQ, LinkedHelper and Outreach.io.

These are some important stats on sales emails, and why tools like these should be critical to your sales strategy:

- McKinsey found that email is 40 times more effective for securing new sales than Facebook and Twitter combined.
- Eighty-six per cent of business professionals prefer email as a communications channel.
- Personalised emails get six times as many transactions.
- Four to seven emails in a sequence can triple your reply rate.
- The ROI on cold emails is twice as high as cold calling.
- Five emails is the ideal number to send.
- Roughly 80 per cent of prospects say 'no' four times before they say yes.
- Fifty per cent of sales happen after the fifth follow-up, yet the average sales rep makes only two attempts to reach a prospect.
- Follow-up emails get a much higher response rate than initial emails. The optimum number of sales call attempts is six.

App	Find out more at	Features and benefits
Lead prospecting and nurturing (*cont'd*)		
VOIQ	voiq.com	• a voicebot platform that makes sales, marketing and customer-support calls for you • qualifies leads, and determines whether or not they have budget, authority, timing and appetite (BANT) to buy • you can integrate it with your CRM and it supports two-way conversations in thousands of voices

Content is King

Quill	narrativescience .com/quill	• a natural language generator that analyses online and digital data to identify the facts, words and language that are important to your sales organisation • produces content that meets your business rules and style preferences like tone, style, formatting and the words you use

Sales monitoring and coaching

Chorus	chorus.ai	• uses artificial intelligence to record, transcribe and analyse sales calls in real time, revealing why deals are won and lost • can break a one-hour call down into a five-minute highlight and provide actionable feedback to help move a prospect forward • can be used to aid knowledge sharing among reps and support the development of training programs that use highlight reels

Sales monitoring and coaching (*cont'd*)

PersistIQ	persistiq.com	• automatically analyses sales activity effectiveness and offers insights and suggestions to sales pros to help them tailor their work • clones successful workflows and improves the sales process
Crystal	crystalknows.com	• gives sales pros personality profiles for everyone they come into contact with • outlines profile information across the web in tools such as LinkedIn, Salesforce and more • access to personality-driven email templates based on the recipient's personality • designed to resonate with recipients, deepening the relationship between the sales pro and customer or prospect

Kissmetrics	kissmetricshq.com	<ul><li>a powerful digital analytics tool</li><li>has event tracking capability that lets you see which webpages individual email list subscribers are landing on, how long they're spending on that page and how many times they've returned</li><li>enables you to set up triggers, so that certain events trigger automatic emails as well</li></ul>
Detective by Charlie	detective.io	<ul><li>does prospect research and supports sales reps tailoring conversations and content accordingly, for example, whether the prospect has been mentioned in the media recently and what for, mutual connections you might have, companies they've worked for in the past</li></ul>
Meeting scheduling		
Clara Labs	claralabs.com	<ul><li>an automated meeting scheduler that uses natural language to respond to email requests, is available 24/7 and follows up automatically with meeting parties</li></ul>

Meeting scheduling (*cont'd*)		
x.ai	x.ai	• enables instant, autonomous meeting scheduling from wherever you work, whether that's email, Slack, your website or your calendar
Calendly	calendly.com	• a calendar scheduling tool that creates your events, sets which timeframes people can book these meetings and then shares the link with people

Marketing tools

If you build it, they will come. Actually, no. As Gabriel Weinberg, author of *Traction*, says, spend 50 per cent of your time on product and 50 per cent on traction (customer acquisition).

Otherwise you'll likely find yourself, like Ray Kinsella (played by Kevin Costner) often did in *Field of Dreams*, staring at an empty baseball field and wondering why 'they' haven't come yet.

Content is huge in today's marketing landscape. If it weren't for content, I doubt my businesses would have won one-quarter of the business we've won. It can be a true differentiator for organisations, especially those with limited resources.

I know first-hand that our 300 plus podcast episodes, 300 plus blog posts and numerous eBooks have been crucial in our reliably generating several hundred leads every month. And by now, you should know that despite limited resources, it's practising the principles of this book that will empower you to create so much content at scale.

But why post just a podcast when you can repurpose it into a blog post, a SlideShare, a YouTube video and more? 'Because that takes time!' you say.

Productivity expert Ari Meisel, founder of Less Doing, developed a content distribution workflow that begins with online service 'repurpose.io' to automatically turn a Facebook Live video into a YouTube video, outputs the audio to podcast services such as Libsyn and SoundCloud, and also to Temi to transcribe the audio to be turned into blog and social media posts, and to SlideShare to create presentations from the content.

If you were to do all of this yourself, it would take you several hours each time, and if you posted just one video a week, that would quickly add up to several hundred hours over the course of the year!

Automation is the kind of thinking you should be applying to your rudimentary, repeatable and process-oriented tasks. First ask, can I automate this, before you even contemplate outsourcing it.

App	Find out more at	Features and benefits
Content		
Repurpose	repurpose.io	• automatically repurposes (surprise surprise!) podcasts, videos and live streams for different platforms to maximise exposure, build brand awareness and boost your sales

ContentFly	contentfly.co	• helps us, at Collective Campus, with the development of eBooks, which we then repurpose as blog posts and podcast episodes
		• we scale our content marketing efforts for a fraction of the cost of writing it ourselves
		• saves hours of editing time by not having to develop content from scratch
Biteable	biteable.com	• assists you in making flashy videos in a snap
Headliner	headliner.app	• generates captioned video files and audiograms in only minutes to promote your product or brand on social media
		• I use this for *Future Squared* podcast audiogram snippets that get shared across LinkedIn, Instagram, Twitter and Facebook
Rev	rev.com	• automatically transcribe audio for you that you can then publish as a blog post, or repurpose into other forms of content
Spext	spext.co	• Spext also supports the development of podcast episodes (for example, importing intro music and voice overs) as well as text-driven audio editing (which removes those annoying ums and ahs from an audio file)

Brill	brill.app	• automatically digitises the content of your notes (for example, sticky notes) and sorts them into pre-determined folders
Google Voice Recorder	Search 'Voice Recorder' in the Google Play store	• records and transcribes voice to text in real time
Speechtexter	speechtexter.com	• free app that records and transcribes voice to text in real time • supports exporting files to Google Docs or Microsoft Word

Email marketing

Vero	getvero.com	• integrates with your CRM and website and uses triggers, based on customer or prospect behaviour, to send relevant, targeted, personalised emails, e.g. if a lead has not moved through the pipeline in a 30-day period, you might send a 'nudge' email to follow up • as of writing, its content management and editing capability leaves a lot to be desired (I'd use something like Mailchimp for simple emails)

Social media marketing

Ribbon	ribbon.social	• re-posts content on social media platforms by extracting interesting excerpts from your content to use as the social media post, increasing engagement*

*For example, figure 13.1 (overleaf) shows a tweet that Ribbon prepared and posted on my behalf, hashtags and all, based on a *Future Squared* episode's RSS feed content.

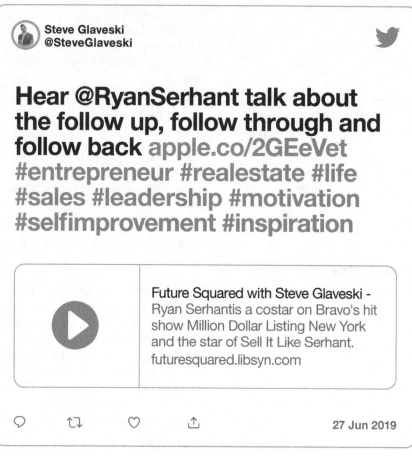

Figure 13.1: automated copy for social media

App	Find out more at	Features and benefits
Social media marketing (*cont'd*)		
RecurPost	recurpost.com	• shares your updates on social media at perfectly timed intervals • helps you post when you get the most engagement based on sophisticated analytics • helps you create variations of your posts so that you can re-share a slightly modified post many times

Marketing automation		
HubSpot	hubspot.com	• provides a full stack of software to help you engage prospects and customers and ultimately grow your business

Other types of automation

Automation extends well beyond the world of sales and marketing alone, to every activity in your company's value chain. Nowadays, almost every business needs to become a technology-driven company, or it could find itself at a serious disadvantage, or out of business altogether.

Finance tools

McKinsey estimates that 27 per cent of finance activities can currently be automated. Nowadays you can use tools to help you automate significant parts of capturing receipts, invoicing clients, performing reconciliations, accepting payments, closing the books, collecting debt, generating management reports, complying with regulations and forecasting. If you or your accounting team are still doing any or all of these tasks completely manually, stop and reflect.

Most modern accounting platforms should support most of the above, whether that be Xero, Zoho Books, MYOB, Oracle NetSuite, Microsoft Dynamics, QuickBooks, FreshBooks, ReceiptBank or others in the space.

IT tools

A Vanson Bourne study found that IT teams spend more than half their time on operations, maintenance and fixing problems. Only 11 per cent say their infrastructure is highly automated.

James Dening from Automation Anywhere told *CIO* magazine that 'IT professionals themselves believe that almost one-fifth of their current daily tasks could be automated by intelligent automation and AI. This could include software or hardware installations, file and folder management, server monitoring, Active Directory management, user on and off-boarding, or batch processing.'

McKinsey also found that 40 to 80 per cent of service desk tickets could and should be automated.

Other aspects of IT that should be subject to automation include device provisioning, security automation, and of course, testing.

Human resources tools

When it comes to HR, automation tools exist along the entire value chain, from workforce planning, to sourcing candidates, interviewing, evaluating, onboarding, monitoring engagement, reviewing performance and offboarding.

For example, a number of tools now have the capacity to shortlist suitable candidates, perform video interviewing and leverage AI to analyse candidate performance, providing you with reports so you can focus your attention on the best candidates, improve your hiring choices and save a lot of time in the process. They can also filter out unconscious bias.

ResearchMoz predicts that the global recruitment software market alone will be worth $2.7 billion by 2022.

Customer support tools

Chatbots such as Collect.chat and virtual agents are perfect for rudimentary, repetitive requests and for customers who prefer self-service which, unsurprisingly perhaps, a growing number of the digital native population has a preference for. Microsoft deploys more than 100 000 virtual agent sessions a day, doubling the number of customers who were able to solve their own problem. HP similarly uses chatbots to handle 70 per cent of its support cases.

Other prominent platforms such as Zendesk, Freshworks, Zoho Desk and HubSpot's Service Hub can automate various aspects of customer support for you.

App	Find out more at	Features and benefits
Customer support		
Voxer	voxer.com	• enables you to listen and respond to voice messages at your convenience • you can use instant voice communication alongside text, photos, video, gifs and share your location • you can also pre-record answers to frequently asked questions and have those answers sent in response to questions received from, say, coaching or consulting clients
Collect.chat	collect.chat	• a simple website widget that empowers you and your team to have conversations with your customers online without having conversations with them • easy to use • helps you to qualify website visitors, increase conversions, answer customer questions and provide support

Workflow optimisation

Here are some workflow-optimisation apps that will help you avoid email rabbit holes.

App	Find out more at	Features and benefits
Send from Gmail (email)	bit.ly/ sendbygmail	• a Google plugin that only opens the compose window so that you circumvent your inbox to avoid distractions and save time

If you need help batch checking email, you can use tools like Inbox Pause (from Gmail extension, Boomerang) to pause incoming email. I hit pause on mine after I check email, and don't hit unpause for several or more hours. Alternatively, you can install the Chrome extension, Block Site, to block access to time drains like Twitter or YouTube during set periods of the day.

App	Find out more at	Features and benefits
Process Street	process.st	• a simple workflow management tool that helps you manage your team's recurring checklists and procedures
		• can be used to support client or employee onboarding, candidate screening, invoice generation, IT support, content promotion and investment due diligence, and so on.

WebMerge	webmerge.me	• a document-generation platform designed to put an end to manual data entry and streamline administrative tasks like the creation and completion of agreements, government forms and sales proposals • integrates with CRM platforms, DocuSign, and online storage platforms like Google Drive and Box

Machine learning is fast becoming a buzzword.

It's one that most people think is the domain of MIT scholars and huge tech companies such as Boston Dynamics only.

This couldn't be further from the truth. While you're not likely to build a Terminator-inspired T-800 — capable of learning empathy — you can build bots to help you get way more done.

If you're interested in learning how to build killer robots, then inquire within your local Department of Defence.

Shaun Hughston, of Agility Automation, has developed a prospect qualification tool using MonkeyLearn and Clearbit to zero in on your ideal customers. Once a new lead enters your database, the tool compares it to your existing customers and gives you an indication as to how likely the lead is to convert.

App	Find out more at	Features and benefits
MonkeyLearn	monkeylearn.com	• helps you to train custom machine learning models to get topic, sentiment, intent, keywords, and so on. • excels at understanding customer insights through support tickets, chats, product reviews, surveys, social media, and so on. • helps you make better customer-centric decisions
Mailparser	mailparser.io	• automatically grabs important data from recurring emails based on your own custom parsing rules • once a new email is processed, your data gets transferred to the business applications you are already using • sends your data to Salesforce or countless other integrations
Zapier and IFTTT (if this then that)	Zapier.com, IFTTT.com	• automate paper-pushing • leverage APIs so App A can talk to App B • support over 1000 apps

At Collective Campus, whenever somebody signs up to our newsletter on our website (Webflow), they are automatically added to our email marketing platform (Vero) and receive an onboarding email. They are automatically added to our CRM (Copper), and I receive a notification about the lead in our instant messaging (Slack) leads channel.

Essentially, these tools help you to automate routine tasks and trigger workflows so that you free up time to work on more important things.

App	Find out more at	Features and benefits
Airtable	airtable.com	• a spreadsheet-database hybrid with the features of a database applied to a spreadsheet • helps you create all sorts of automations that select and join disparate parts of different documents, for example, combining slides from different proposals into one proposal
Phantombuster	phantombuster.com	• a suite of ready-to-go APIs to crank up your marketing, for example, it can auto-comment on LinkedIn posts, find people's emails and extract contacts from Facebook
ScrapeStorm	scrapestorm.com	• automatically extracts data from websites without having to write any code

Scripts and custom tools

We've developed a number of scripts at Collective Campus that leverage multiple tools in order to streamline key business activities that would otherwise take hours to perform. Over the course of the year, they save us thousands of hours — and we're not a big team.

Chances are, if you can imagine it, you can build them (or better yet, get somebody to build them for you!).

Prospect outreach

We use a combination of LinkedIn's Sales Navigator, Phantombuster, LeadIQ, Heroku and SendGrid to find prospects using search terms. These tools extract their email addresses and facilitate personalised emails.

Aside from creating the initial search definitions and the email copy, the process is completed automatically using a custom app and the APIs of each platform, and is run periodically on a set schedule.

Canned responses

Do you find yourself typing out the same kinds of emails, over and over again? As Ari Meisel says, every time you find yourself saying 'every', that's your cue to automate. 'Canned responses' is a Gmail feature that enables users to create and save multiple email templates in their inbox. When you need to type up another follow-up email, you just click a button, and you're done.

You can also use tools like PasteAway and PhraseExpress on Windows, Mac, iOS and Android devices.

Machine learning outreach

We use a combination of Airtable, SendGrid, Zapier and Crunchbase to identify prospects who fit a specific criteria, based on the profile of our existing customer database. We also use a similar tool to identify both facilitators/consultants and startups that we'd like to work with in our business.

Proposal automation

Having spent years at large consulting firms, I saw consultants painstakingly labour over proposals for days, if not weeks, often recreating them from the ground up.

At Collective Campus, we use a script we've built to automatically generate proposals. We use a combination of Airtable and WebMerge to enter custom information for a proposal, select relevant template sections, and have the final PowerPoint document generated, complete with the prospect's logo and brand colour schemes.

Some customisation may be required, but you end up spending 80 to 90 per cent less time preparing the proposal. When you consider that my company submits 200 or so proposals a year, this saves us serious time. Find out more at quickprop.io.

List scraping

I've used lists in many ways to further my business and creative pursuits.

In the build-up to the release of my previous book, *Employee to Entrepreneur*, I used list building to formulate and automatically target a list of podcast hosts and make a case for appearing on their show to talk about the book. I ended up appearing on more than 50, including big podcasts such as *Mixergy* and *Sell or Die*.

When there's a big tech or innovation conference happening, I'll use list building to put together a list of the speakers and attendees tweeting on social media. I'll then contact them with a targeted message: 'Missed you at Conference X!' This gets a conversation going with people who are engaging in our domain and more likely to respond.

But rather than manually do this—you guessed it—we use tools like Mailparser to help us automate the process. Find out more at mailparser.io.

Onboarding new hires and contract bots

Given that we subscribe to the business model map for the new economy—which I introduced in chapter 2—we tend to work with a lot of talent on demand. But using talent on demand is difficult and costly if the onboarding process is slow, and the cost of the back and forth communication is high.

As such, we use a combination of JotForm, Zapier, Airtable, WebMerge and SendGrid to automate this.

When we bring on a contractor for the first time, they go through an online workflow that runs them through everything they need to know. There they will also find a downloadable template for a workshop, and they can upload their version for review. We'll get notified via email of any updates or incomplete steps, and follow-up emails will be triggered accordingly.

This saves us a heck of a lot of time onboarding people, and makes it as seamless as possible and easier to scale our talent on-demand model.

Twitter lead gen

When *HBR* published my '6-Hour Workday' article, the interwebs exploded (at least that's what it looked like from where I was sitting!). Various outlets such as *The Wall Street Journal*, *The Daily Mail*, CNBC, News.com.au and *The New Zealand Herald* picked it up. *HBR*'s tweets of the article all received several hundred retweets and hundreds of likes — but they were engaging with *HBR*'s brand and social, not mine.

So what did I do about this?

We built a workflow using a customer API in Phantombuster plus Followers DM to scrape the Twitter handles and send personalised Twitter messages. Now, not everybody receives the message, depending on their settings, but many do, and it's far better than none. We pointed them to other similar content we've published that might be of interest, and they are incentivised to opt-in to our mailing list. Find out more at followersdm.com.

Bonus round: I feel the need, the need for speed

Much of the content we consume, be it film, movies or podcasts, can often run at a slower pace than it needs to.

Everybody is familiar with speeding up podcasts and audio books, but what about documentaries, films and that latest Netflix special you want to watch? Well, you can have your cake and eat it too. To avoid spending too much time consuming, install the Chrome Video Speed Controller plugin (equivalents exist for other browsers). This allows you to speed up any online video service (including Netflix!). It's not an automation tool as such, but it will serve the same purpose and save you time.

For example, I tend to watch many documentaries and films on about 1.3 times. It doesn't sound like much, but let's do the maths:

Time Saving = Duration - (Duration/Speed)

A 90-minute film at 1.3 speed means you can watch it in just 70 minutes. That's a 20-minute saving!

Sometimes, depending on the production, I can comfortably watch video at 1.5 times, without materially affecting the experience, which brings a 90-minute production down to just 60 minutes!

It quickly adds up. This is *especially* important if you like to catch a film before you head off to sleep but find yourself staying up longer than you should, and sacrificing your sleep and performance the next day.

I'm willing to trade in a dramatic pause here and there if it means I get an extra 30 minutes of sleep.

CALL TO ACTION

1. Which of your tasks can you automate? Reflect on table 13.1.

2. Make a list of the tools mentioned that can benefit you; sign up to them/install them and implement your time-saving automations today.

3. Speed up your videos next time you watch Netflix or your favourite streaming service.

CHAPTER 14

O: Outsource (and delegate)

In the 1830s, Charles Babbage pioneered the concept of a programmable computer.

One hundred and sixty years later, in 1991, his design was assembled by a museum...and it worked!

But that wasn't Babbage's only significant contribution to the world. The Babbage Principle declared that highly skilled, high-cost labourers shouldn't be doing the low-skilled work that should be done by low-cost labourers.

Babbage noted that highly skilled workers were spending part of their time on jobs that were more suited to lower-paid workers. Employers weren't getting dollar-for-dollar value when it came to highly skilled worker pay because they were paying for skills that weren't being utilised.

He suggested that employers could get more value by dividing labour, and by matching worker skillsets with the jobs to be done.

This principle went on to characterise the division of labour and the distribution of wealth during the remainder of the Industrial Revolution.

Almost two centuries later, Babbage's principle seems forgotten—whether it's six-figure-earning professionals labouring over the positioning of a table in a PowerPoint proposal, or an entrepreneur spending hours reconciling transactions in their accounting software.

QUESTION TO PONDER

Are you doing things that people can do for a fraction of your hourly rate? If so, consider that every hour you spend on such tasks is actually costing you money by way opportunity cost.

Process-oriented tasks that can't be automated should, at the very least, be delegated or outsourced.

Author and marketing consultant Perry Marshall put forward a table of tasks based on per-hour rates (see table 14.1) in his book, *80/20 Sales and Marketing*.

Table 14.1: $10-an-hour to $10 000-an-hour tasks

$10 per hour	$100 per hour	$1000 per hour	$10 000 per hour
Running errands	Solving a problem for a prospective or existing customer	Planning and prioritising your day	Improving your USP
Talking to unqualified prospects	Talking to a qualified prospect	Negotiating with a qualified prospect	Creating new and better offers
Cold calling (of any variety)	Writing an email to prospects or customers	Building your sales funnel	Re-positioning your message and position
Building and fixing stuff on your website	Creating marketing tests and experiments	Judging marketing tests and experiments	Executing 'bolt from the blue' brilliant ideas
Doing expense reports	Managing Pay-Per-Click campaigns	Creating Pay-Per-Click campaigns	Negotiating major deals

$10 per hour	$100 per hour	$1000 per hour	$10 000 per hour
Working 'social media' the way most people do it	Doing social media well (this is rare)	Doing social media with extreme competence (this is very rare)	Selling to high-value customers and groups
Cleaning, sorting	Outsourcing simple tasks	Delegating complex tasks	Selecting team members
Attending meetings	Customer follow-up	Writing sales copy	Public speaking

Source: Perry Marshall, *80/20 Sales and Marketing*

'But I'm an entrepreneur with a team of two and I can't afford to outsource!'

Actually, you can't afford not to outsource, especially because you're a resource-strapped team of two.

AngelList founder Naval Ravikant suggests setting an aspirational hourly rate for yourself and sticking to it.

'Never do anything with your time for less than that amount — whether it's attending a meeting or returning a package from Amazon...If I have to return something, and it costs less than my personal hourly rate, I'll throw or give it away.'

If you can hire someone for less than your hourly rate, do it.

If you truly value your time, you'll focus only on tasks worth at least $100 and above.

The cost of not doing so is far greater than the $10 you save doing it yourself.

Having worked with hundreds of entrepreneurs, I often present them with the information in table 14.1 and ask, 'What percentage of your time do you spend on $10-an-hour tasks?'

Most respond with something to the order of half their time.

When I press them on why they don't invest more time into outsourcing their rudimentary and repeatable tasks, they respond without a hint of irony, 'I don't have time to do that!'

I've outsourced about 40 hours a week of tasks that I had previously performed myself, without any noticeable decrease in quality (and sometimes an improvement). That's a standard 9-to-5 week worth of tasks!

But the real value isn't just in the time I save.

It's in freeing me up to invest my time, and cognition, into high-value tasks that align with my strengths. This creates more value than repeatable process-oriented tasks and it means better results that feed back into my motivation to invest my time. And so the cycle goes on.

If you find yourself doing all manner of monotonous tasks on top of your value-adding tasks, then you're likely to find it much harder to keep going and stay enthusiastic about your work because it feels like, well, work.

Nowadays, there can be no excuse for not outsourcing rudimentary tasks that can't be automated. Numerous platforms can get you up and running.

You can outsource not just professional tasks, but personal tasks that don't deliver you any value or joy. Doing so will free up both mental and physical energy for work, life and play.

Hate mowing the lawn, but you currently devote two hours a month to it? If your hourly rate is $100 and you can get someone to mow the lawn for $50, then hire them.

For some, mowing the lawn may be a form of therapy, and that's fine.

Don't outsource it if it brings you joy.

When to outsource

People often ask me, 'What and when should I outsource?'

There's no right answer to this question. We're all dealing with a collection of competing considerations, so reflecting on the following should help you to make a more informed decision:

- the cost of outsourcing
- the urgency of the task

- whether it's a recurring task
- whether the task can be automated
- whether it's mission critical
- whether there's an IP or privacy risk
- whether it's a specialist or commodity task
- whether it aligns with your strengths
- whether you're doing something you enjoy
- whether it has the potential for serendipity.

The cost of outsourcing

If it's going to cost you or your organisation $1000 to perform a task, you'll want to consider outsourcing it—if you can get it done well for less outside the building.

When considering the cost, don't stop at the fee you pay a contractor for their services.

You should also account for the total cost of searching, evaluating, hiring, onboarding, instructing, monitoring and managing.

Consider direct fees for hiring plus your own time by calculating internal hourly rates × number of hours required to perform the aforementioned tasks.

Most critically, don't discount the *opportunity* cost of what you could be doing if you didn't outsource a task. It may be cheaper to do it internally, but it may prevent you from performing higher value tasks.

The urgency of the task

If you've got a proposal that's due in two days, you could outsource it. But you run the risk of it not being done in time. You'll want to factor in the time required to find, onboard and instruct someone to perform the task, and review the work before it goes out.

Urgent tasks may lend themselves to outsourcing to *existing* contractors who understand your business and the work that needs to be performed. New resources may struggle to perform the task correctly in time.

Is it a recurring task?

If it's a one-off task, you might consider doing it internally. This doesn't apply if the one-off task will take weeks to perform and the cost of outsourcing it is less than the cost of doing it yourself.

Can the task be automated?

If the task is repeatable and can be automated, don't outsource it. It will save you a tonne of money and time in human effort, and also remove the risk of human error.

Is it mission-critical?

If you're in the business of shoe manufacturing, then supply chains, order taking, shipping and finance are all mission-critical. This extends to tasks that carry significant business risk such as security and privacy.

You'll want to pay top dollar to ensure these mission-critical tasks are done correctly. But it's not always necessary to keep these tasks inside the building.

It comes down to quality, speed and cost. For example, a website with strong user experience (UX) is mission-critical to our work at Collective Campus because the website serves as a primary source of lead generation, social proof and ultimately, sales. However, web design is not aligned with our strengths at Collective Campus.

We outsource it and pay top dollar to get experts working with us as a result. However, this is far cheaper than having a full-time UXer in-house 365 days a year.

On the other hand, developing workshop content is mission-critical and aligns with our strengths and core purpose. As a result, we do it ourselves, or partner with reputable third parties we trust to co-create it.

You'll want to determine whether or not you can outsource mission-critical tasks in a way that doesn't fundamentally compromise quality.

If it compromises customer satisfaction, retention and referrals, tread carefully. If you're in doubt, run some experiments, and if all of your experiments fail, do the tasks internally.

Is there an IP or privacy risk?

Some questions to ask when considering privacy are:

- What's the risk and can we accept that level of risk? (see figure 14.1)
- Can we sanitise the documents?
- Are we bound by any regulatory requirements?
- Can we put into place and enforce confidentiality agreements?

		Consequence				
		Insignificant	Minor	Moderate	Major	Severe
	Almost certain	Medium	High	High	Extreme	Extreme
Likelihood	Likely	Medium	Medium	High	Extreme	Extreme
	Possible	Low	Medium	Medium	High	Extreme
	Unlikely	Low	Low	Medium	High	High
	Rare	Low	Low	Low	Medium	High

Figure 14.1: a risk matrix

Is it a specialist or commodity task?

Commodity services are more likely to be outsourced because, by their nature, they have been commodified and can be performed cheaply outside the building.

Alignment with your strengths

One of my business philosophies is to focus on my strengths. No matter how much you work on addressing your weaknesses, there are going to be people out there who excel in that area. Whatever time you spend coding, even though you're mediocre at it, is time you don't spend selling, which is where your strengths may lie.

Look at it this way.

If you have two marketing channels and one generates $2 for every $1 you spend, while the other generates $3, every dollar you spend on the former is actually costing you money.

You should exhaust the $3 channel first. Then you can reallocate the returns generated into other opportunities.

The same goes for how you choose to spend your time.

Being good at playing hopscotch doesn't mean you should devote all of your waking hours to it (unless your goal in life is to become the world hopscotch champion). Apply reason.

On commodities:

Just because you're strong at something, it doesn't mean that you should continue to do it if it is available as a commodity function elsewhere.

For example, if a shoe manufacturer has a solid IT department running an efficient data centre, it doesn't mean that it should continue to follow that model. In the long term, moving to a commodity cloud provider can provide better flexibility and reduced costs.

Strengths stop being strengths once the competitive advantage is gone.

Do what you enjoy

You may want to continue to do work you enjoy because it feeds into your morale and wellbeing. However, you'll want to stay clear of what

Behance founder Scott Belsky calls 'insecurity work'. This refers to all of the things you are repeatedly doing that aren't moving the needle forward, but you keep doing just to assure yourself that everything is okay. Think checking your mentions, social, analytics, sales, email and so on.

I enjoy blogging, but it's hard to draw a straight line between the number of blogs penned and sales generated. As such, I don't devote *all of my time* to blogging. I limit it to about four blogs a month, which accounts for several hours of time.

If you enjoy it and it aligns with your competitive advantage, then yes, keep doing it. But decrease your investment or kill it if it isn't moving the needle.

The potential for serendipity

Creativity is essentially the connecting of disparate ideas.

Austin Kleon, author of *Steal Like an Artist*, says that every artist he spoke to confessed that they 'stole' their ideas. Or, more accurately speaking, they build upon and connect the ideas of others before them.

The same holds true in teams. By bringing people together with disparate ideas, you're setting foundations for creativity and new ideas to emerge.

The risk of outsourcing all kinds of tasks and keeping your core team relatively small, with a small set of interdisciplinary skills, is that creativity and innovation suffer as a result.

To help allay you of this risk, create a mechanism for sharing ideas with external parties. Bring contractors, partners, clients and externals into strategy and brainstorming sessions and design sprints.

While there are many permutations, table 14.2 (overleaf) aims to provide clarity on some of the most common outsourcing dilemmas you may find yourself in.

Table 14.2: when to outsource

Repeat/ one-off	Urgent/ not urgent	Automate/ can't automate	Cheaper to outsource/ more expensive to outsource	You enjoy it/ you hate It	Strength/ weakness
Repeat	Not urgent	Can't automate	Cheaper	Hate it	Weakness
Repeat	Not urgent	Can't automate	Cheaper	Hate it	Weakness
Repeat	Not urgent	Can't automate	Cheaper	Hate it	Strength
Repeat	Not urgent	Automate	Cheaper	Hate it	Weakness
Repeat	Not urgent	Can't automate	More expensive	Hate it	Weakness
Repeat	Not urgent	Can't automate	Cheaper	Hate it	Weakness
Not repeatable	Urgent	Can't automate	Cheaper	Hate it	Weakness
Repeat	Not urgent	Can't automate	Cheaper	Enjoy it	Weakness

Commodity/ specialist	Mission-critical	Quality compromised to unacceptable level/not compromised	Business risk compromised to unacceptable level/not compromised	Compromises serendipity and creativity	Result
Commodity	Yes	Not compromised	Not compromised	No	Outsource
Commodity	Yes	Compromised	Not compromised	No	Do internally
Commodity	Yes	Not compromised	Not compromised	Yes	Outsource but have a process to engineer outside input into internal design sprints, brainstorming sessions etc.
Commodity	Yes	Not compromised	Not compromised	No	Automate
Commodity	Yes	Not compromised	Not compromised	No	Do internally, but outsource if the opportunity cost on your time is greater, and you can afford to do so
Specialist	Yes	Not compromised	Not compromised	No	Outsource to specialist
Specialist	Yes	Not compromised	Not compromised	No	Do internally
Commodity	Yes	Not compromised	Not compromised	No	Outsource, but do occasionally internally if you enjoy it and good for morale

Watch out!

Be careful who you outsource to. If you outsource consulting work, you've got to first, trust and second, incentivise contractors so that they don't steal your clients away.

Pay premium for strategy, not for execution

You would be forgiven for thinking that outsourcing is all about cutting costs and getting people outside of your company to do rudimentary work for bargain-basement prices.

It also extends to just the opposite: paying top-of-market prices.

As Scott Belsky puts it, 'While you should probably never outsource your competitive advantage, sometimes the perfect designer or other domain expert insists on working on their own as a freelancer.'

When something is mission-critical, but not a strength, you have two choices:

1. Hire a superstar to add to your team and pay them accordingly.
2. Outsource to a gun freelancer and pay them accordingly.

Say I need a gun digital-marketer to run our company's SEO and search engine marketing (SEM) function.

I could hire and pay six figures.

I could outsource and pay six figures.

But, there's a third choice that gives me superior outcomes at a fraction of the price.

Building on the distinction between commodity and specialist work, I would outsource the strategy work to a gun SEO consultant, and outsource the execution of the consultant's recommendations for a fraction of the rate.

Almost anybody can be trained to move widgets around. Knowing which widgets to move around in the first place is much more difficult.

My general rule of thumb is to pay top dollar for strategy and bargain-basement prices for implementation of recommendations, especially where almost anybody with some basic training can do the work.

I have no qualms about paying several hundred dollars an hour for marketing, sales or SEO experts.

While the hourly cost may be high, we're tapping into expert talent and only have to pay them for the duration of the project, which is often short.

Instead of paying $100 000 a year for a full-time run-of-the-mill digital marketer, you may end up paying $5000 to $10 000 upfront for some quality advisory work, and another $15 000 for the execution, not only saving you 75 per cent, or over $75 000 a year, but creating way more value by way of the results delivered on a campaign. It's a win–win.

What about small tasks?

You might think that small tasks are too small to bother outsourcing, but remember, if it's a repeatable task—and a repeatable task that multiple people in your team partake in—then the time taken up doing it can add up very quickly. Not only that, but we've already addressed the cost of task-switching (in chapter 10), which comes at the expense of flow and higher level critical thinking—key to success in today's knowledge economy.

Small tasks add up; just look at table 14.3 (overleaf) to determine how much time your team could be saving.

Even a one-minute task carried out five times a day adds up to a three-day saving *per year*, if outsourced—not accounting for opportunity or task-switching cost.

Table 14.3: outsourcing small tasks saves you big time

How long it takes	How often your team collectively does it							
	50 times a day	25 times a day	5 times a day	daily	weekly	monthly	quarterly	yearly
10 seconds	4.8 days	2.4 days	3.75 hours	45 minutes	9 minutes	2 minutes	40 seconds!	10 seconds!
1 minute	28.8 days	14.4 days	3 days	4.5 hours	54 minutes	15 minutes	4 minutes	1 minute
5 minutes	144 days	72 days	15 days	3 days	4.5 hours	1.1 hours	20 minutes	5 minutes
30 minutes	864 days	432 days	90 days	18 days	3.6 days	1 day	2 hours	30 minutes
1 hour	1728 days	864 days	173 days	36 days	7.2 days	2 days	4 hours	1 hour
4 hours	6912 days	3456 days	692 days	144 days	29 days	4 days	1.3 days	2 hours
1 day	41 472 days	20 736 days	4147 days	864 days	174 days	24 days	8 days	12 hours

If you have five people engaged in such tasks, the saving is 15 days, which at an average daily rate of $400, saves you or your organisation $6000.

Do your staff each spend an hour a month completing expense reports? Outsourcing the process will save them two days a year, and if you have 100 staff, that saves your organisation 200 days a year, or $80000 using the $400 day rate mentioned previously.

The cost of taking the time to set up outsourcing usually pays itself off well within the first year.

How to manage remote resources

It has never been easier to build and manage a globally distributed team of resources.

There are numerous project and team management tools on the market.

But before you even get to that point, you'll want to be clear about:

- the purpose of the role and the position description
- the instructions
- the metrics of success.

Want to ensure that your remote team pull their weight? Well, you could micromanage them, but this defeats the purpose and only creates monotonous work for you, while destroying morale for them.

Start by getting the right people on the bus.

Perform reference checks, ask the right questions during interviews, implement probationary periods and refer to past feedback if sourcing them from an online marketplace such as Freelancer.

Once you've found the right person, and clearly communicated what they need to do, you can use tools such as Asana or Trello to manage tasks, and instant messaging platforms such as Slack to communicate.

Like an internal team member, you'll want to make sure that remote resources are incentivised to perform and that you treat them like part of a team. Sending them a gift on their birthday or a goofy team video via Slack goes a long way.

In terms of making them feel like the team, you could invest in an annual retreat, whether that be a regional or global get-together. Basecamp has over 50 employees but only 14 of these are in Chicago; the rest are globally distributed. Once a year, Basecamp hosts a global retreat that brings everybody together to build face-to-face relationships and camaraderie. Companies such as Automattic, Zapier and Buffer are following suit.

Out of sight shouldn't mean out of mind, but it shouldn't mean always on your mind either. If you set up the right systems, and onboard the right people, you should have no more issues managing a remote workforce than you would a local one.

Types of tasks you can outsource

Here's a short but inexhaustible list of tasks that can be outsourced:

- content creation, curation and distribution
- bookkeeping
- payroll
- conversion optimisation
- reporting
- scheduling and administrative tasks
- research
- data entry
- presentations
- graphic design
- web design and development
- call answering
- email management
- social media marketing and influencer outreach
- podcast guest shortlisting, outreach and scheduling
- podcast editing, mixing, publishing and distribution
- conference speaking opportunity outreach
- lead generation and qualification of prospects

- video development
- analytics reporting.

At its core, anything that can be effectively codified into a clear, actionable, step-by-step process — and doesn't come with unacceptable privacy, intellectual capital or quality risks — should be outsourced.

The insourcing fallacy

Nowadays, there's a trend for organisations to declare that 'outsourcing doesn't work' and that they are 'insourcing' instead.

But, like any tool, outsourcing is only as good as *how* you use it.

You wouldn't expect a permanent hire to succeed in their role without a sufficient onboarding and training protocol, so why would you expect a lone warrior sitting halfway across the world, who you've never physically met before, to do any better?

You've got to be explicit with your instructions. Don't leave anything to chance. As Toltec spiritualist and author Don Miguel Ruiz put it in *The Four Agreements*, 'Don't make assumptions.'

Don't leave any rocks unturned if you expect your hired gun to deliver what you envisage in the dark recesses of your mind.

For example, my process document for podcast guest outreach is about 14 pages long. It's a 2000-word Google doc with 12-point font, complete with screenshots, arrows, bubbles and captions!

Outsourcing tools

Nowadays, there are numerous tools on the market that make it so much easier to find, onboard, instruct and manage outsourcees or remote assistants.

Personal assistant

'I forgot my credit card at the bar. Can you send someone to pick it up and deliver it to my apartment?'

'Can you book me a flight for the Atlanta conference? Try to get me an upgrade with my usual rewards program.'

'Can you log in and respond to our customer support Zendesk emails every day from 5 pm to 8 am?'

These are the kinds of requests that you can literally text apps such as Magic (getmagic.com).

Magic learns about your work and life, remembers your preferences, logs into your accounts, and interacts with your friends and co-workers as your very own dedicated assistant.

Odd jobs

Tools such as TaskRabbit (taskrabbit.com) essentially help you find people for all sorts of odd jobs, whether they be lawnmowing, cleaning and removals, IT support, furniture assembly or handy work around the house.

I found somebody on Airtasker (airtasker.com) to collect almost 100, six-kilogram boxes of paperback books from my team's old office, deliver them to my house and store them in my spare bedroom's wardrobe! This task was completed within just three hours of requesting it, and cost me just $80.

This was way less than what my combined hourly rate would have amounted to. If I had done this myself it would have taken me at least twice as long. I didn't have the necessary equipment or vehicle, and so it would have cost me multiple trips, put me at risk of physical injury and come at a significant opportunity cost (I would have lost an entire day).

Given that I value my time at more than $13 an hour, this was a no brainer.

Creative freelancers and virtual assistants

Platforms such as Freelancer (freelancer.com), Upwork (upwork.com) and Airtasker (airtasker.com) are great for onboarding contractors for creative work as well as finding virtual assistants.

Whether it's web or mobile development, design work, writing, marketing, inside sales, customer service, podcast production or video editing, platforms such as these can hook you up with talented creatives to get the job done, often for less than $10 an hour depending on the type of task.

Of course, as with any change to the way you currently do things, you'll go through an inevitable period of testing and tweaking. Knowing how to do this well, so that you optimise your time and effort, forms the basis of the next chapter.

CALL TO ACTION

1. Determine your aspirational hourly rate.

2. Take stock of your $10-an-hour tasks and get to work preparing a process document and outsourcing them.

3. Review the tools presented in this chapter, and experiment with using them for your professional and personal tasks—thank me later.

4. Determine which of your weaknesses you should be outsourcing.

5. Apply the outsourcing calculation to your repeatable tasks, and any tasks that land on your desk.

6. Review the list of tasks that can be outsourced. Determine what else you should outsource that wasn't identified as part of steps 2 to 5 (*note:* this could extend to tasks you haven't started doing because you had no time, money or expertise, but you now realise you can outsource to professionals online for a shadow of what you had previously expected to pay).

CHAPTER 15
T: Test and iterate

'LAUNCH'

The Soviet Union's missile attack warning system displayed the verb in a large, red font.

This was a very reliable system, and the message was being relayed to Stanislav Petrov, a Soviet Lieutenant Colonel sitting at the control panel.

The system informed Petrov that a US missile was on its way to the USSR. In fact, *five* ballistic US missiles were reported to be on their way. The Soviet nuclear doctrine called for immediate and full nuclear retaliation in such circumstances.

The Reagan administration had been deploying Pershing II missiles capable of striking the Soviet Union to West Germany and Great Britain. All signs pointed to this being a legitimate nuclear strike by the United States on the USSR.

But Petrov did not report the incoming strike.

It turned out that the system had confused the sun's reflection off clouds for a missile. The Soviets and the Americans collectively had over 59 000 nuclear warheads.

On 26 September 1983, Petrov prevented a nuclear holocaust.

★ ★ ★

One of the most common pitfalls that people fall into is jumping to conclusions. They over-invest time, energy and/or money into the wrong pursuit, one that extracts a lot more value than it ends up generating.

If Petrov had jumped to conclusions, the world today might be nothing but barren land.

The other major pitfall is analysis paralysis: wasting resources pontificating and essentially doing nothing at all. But to succeed in both business and life, we usually need to take action — and like Petrov, it needs to be *the right action*.

Peter Drucker purportedly said that 'there's nothing worse than the wrong things done right'.

So how do we increase our chances of taking the right action?

Well, in an environment of high uncertainty, we need to optimise for diversity. Just like a mining company engaged in prospecting small-scale mineral exploration on a large scale to find commercially viable ore deposits, we need to become adept at placing lots of small bets. We must get better at measuring the results to learn what we should do more of, and what we should do less of. We must adjust our thinking and behaviour accordingly.

Metrics that matter

The first rule of analytics is to measure what matters — not to measure everything.

The US National Security Agency (NSA) knows a thing or two about measuring too much. Former NSA official William Binney has said that the agency has become 'so engorged with data that they are no longer effective, losing vital intelligence in the fray. An analyst today can run one simple query across the NSA's various databases, only to become immediately overloaded with information'.

The NSA watches over about two-thirds of the world's population so there is a huge amount of data being collected.

Binney maintains that this is why they were unable to prevent the Boston bombing or the Paris shootings, even though the data was all there. Essentially, they were unable to find the needle in the haystack.

You should identify and measure only what matters so that you're not left with the same problem, and the quality of your decisions doesn't suffer as a result.

Whatever the function, there will always be metrics that matter.

For sales, you may be most concerned with leads generated, qualified, met with, converted and the total dollar value of those conversions.

For marketing, you may be concerned with new website visitors, newsletter sign-ups and returning visitors.

For customer support, you may be concerned with the number of queries, average wait times, time to resolve queries, and, ultimately, your net promoter score.

While there may be hundreds of metrics we can measure across these areas, these may be your key top-level metrics.

For example, if Airbnb wanted to monitor the quality of its performance as an organisation, there would no doubt be hundreds of potential metrics they could measure. But if they had to pick just two, what do you think they would be?

Let's reflect on the mission of the company:

... live in the world where one day you can feel like you're home anywhere & not in a home, but truly home, where you belong.

Essentially, the company provides a lodging service so people can stay in homes rather than hotels all over the world.

Based on this, it becomes apparent that you would measure the number of nights booked and perhaps the number of nights returned—the latter an indication of the quality of experience you had using the platform.

Everything else is a sub-metric to these guiding lights.

Focus on the metrics that will represent the greatest consequence to you or your work, should they underperform.

For example, I introduced the data in table 15.1 in my book *Employee to Entrepreneur* to help would-be entrepreneurs identify and test the assumptions that truly matter.

You can use a similar model to identify which metrics you should concern yourself with.

It works like this:

- *A:* determine the impact out of 10 on your work if the metric underperforms.
- *B:* how certain are you that this metric will perform consistently/how volatile is it?

Divide A by B to get your result, and prioritise by the higher number. Use this to inform which metrics are worth tracking, and which are just sub-metrics that are reflections of the key metrics and aren't saying anything new.

Table 15.1: how to prioritise assumptions

	Step 1					Step 2		
	Low 0	High 10	Low 0	High 10	#	Today 1	Future 5	Rank
	Impact		Certainty			Time		
Assumption 1	9		3		3	2		1.5
Assumption 2	8		4		2	3		0.66
Assumption 3	7		5		1.4	4		0.35

Frequency of measurement

So, how often should you measure your progress? Well, that comes down to how volatile and fast-changing your particular domain is. You may want to review some metrics daily; and others weekly, monthly or quarterly. Anything beyond this and you're leaving yourself open to very long feedback loops and not adapting fast enough to changing circumstances.

Additionally, there may be external or internal incidents or events that warrant checking the impact on metrics. These may include external technological, societal, economic or political factors, as well as internal changes, campaigns or issues raised—all of which may have an effect on performance.

When my team publishes a new eBook, we pay close attention to the number of new visitors we have on our site. More importantly, the number of new leads generated by eBook downloads. If we don't check in on this early, all of our efforts developing the eBook may be for naught as download numbers remain low. Checking in early gives us the data we need to take affirmative action and interject. Perhaps we need to explore some alternative distribution channels. Perhaps we need to target some different keywords. Perhaps the title of the eBook needs to change to something a little more compelling...and so on.

It's easy to confuse motion with progress, so by measuring performance, we spend more time learning and moving forward, and less time doing things just because that's how they've always been done.

CALL TO ACTION

Whenever you're embarking on an uncertan pursuit:

1. Define your assumptions.
2. Prioritise your assumptions using the table provided.
3. Define the metrics that matter.
4. Test your assumptions and gather key metrics.
5. Learn from the metrics, and adapt accordingly.

Remember to keep the feedback loop short to accelerate learning and minimise wastage.

CHAPTER 16
S: Start your engine

There's a beautiful excerpt from Marcus Aurelius's journals, released under the guise of *Meditations*, that I've long been a fan of. In part it reads,

> At dawn, when you have trouble getting out of bed, tell yourself: I have to go to work... What do I have to complain of, if I'm going to do what I was born for...? Or is this what I was created for? To huddle under the blankets and stay warm?

It points to our biologically ingrained desire to conserve energy, to take the path of least resistance, to do what is most comfortable, such as stay in bed longer.

Steven Pressfield spoke of this phenomenon in his book *The War of Art*, and dubbed that little voice in our heads urging us to take the high road, 'resistance':

> Never forget: This very moment, we can change our lives. There never was a moment, and never will be, when we are without the power to alter our destiny. This second we can turn the tables on resistance. This second, we can sit down and do our work.

From a biological perspective, you could say that human beings are hard-wired for laziness. Professor Daniel Lieberman, an evolutionary biologist at Harvard University, claims that to conserve energy in hard times, evolution predisposes us to do as little exercise as required.

Writing in a paper for *Current Sports Medicine Reports*, Lieberman explained that,

> because humans evolved to be active for play or necessity, efforts to promote exercise will require altering environments in ways that nudge or even compel people to be active and to make exercise fun.

This ties in with what we discussed in chapter 11. By doing what you're naturally predisposed to, what you enjoy and what generates results, you're more likely to enjoy the play of work.

However, your physiology is urging you to watch the latest episode of *Black Mirror*, check your email for the umpteenth time or mindlessly scroll through Instagram instead.

So, how do we go about overwriting tens of thousands of years of evolution, and get to work?

In this chapter, I put forward proven techniques that you can begin to apply today by starting your engine to get vastly better tomorrow. A 1 per cent improvement every day is all it takes to become 37 times better by the end of the year.

Combine these techniques with the flow triggers presented in chapter 3.

Create the right environment

As we've already established, once you're interrupted, getting back into the zone is no easy feat, taking about 23 minutes. So you must create an environment where you *won't* be interrupted, especially if you're engaged in heuristic work.

First, it's unlikely that your organisation has a culture where colleagues can't book time in your calendar. If my assumption is true, block your own time out in advance. Strive to have at least two hours a day, if not more, where you will be completely uninterrupted, and align this time with your chronotype, introduced in chapter 4.

As an early bird, I do most of my best and deep work in the mornings, so I make sure this time is mine (nobody can book time in my calendar in the mornings).

Second, shut off notifications on both your desktop and mobile phone. Jason Fried, co-founder at Basecamp, has turned off all desktop and smartphone notifications and sets his phone to Airplane mode most of the time. Only significant people, such as his wife, are able to get through. Doing so gives him time to focus and get several hours of deep work in each day.

Third, put yourself in an environment where it's unlikely you'll be interrupted. Unless you've got a culture where people respect your flow, you'll need to lock yourself away somewhere that's conducive to flow. One where you'll be unlikely to get tapped on the shoulder every 15 minutes, or sucked into conversations about the last episode of *Game of Thrones*.

Fourth, close any browser windows that are going to distract you. For example, that LinkedIn or inbox window probably doesn't need to be there. Our brains are wired to pull that slot machine lever and find out if we'll get triple cherries. Chances are, you'll be tempted to check social or email if those browser windows stay open. Close them. Out of sight, out of mind.

If you find this difficult, you can go a step further and install the Freedom app or Block Site, and block access to specific applications for scheduled periods. You can even set this to automatically block these applications during your designated flow time each day.

Physiology and mental state

We can't talk about the mind without talking about the body, and vice versa. While there seems to be a false dichotomy in society when talking of body and mind, the two are interwoven. As we've established, our microbiota, or our gut, may affect not only the decisions we make about what to eat and drink, but also the people we choose to spend time with, and the way we assess critical information.

Additionally, it turns out that cognitive games, or 'brain games', don't actually make you smarter. They only make you better at playing the games the more you do them. The best exercise for your mind is actually the same exercise you do for your body. So if you want to get smarter, heed the words of Seneca and engage in some 'running, brandishing weights, or jumping'.

Yes...jumping.

Stress

Too stressed to be productive?

Take a look at figure 16.1. According to the Yerkes-Dodson law, performance increases with physiological or mental arousal (stress), but only up to a point. When the level of stress becomes too high, performance decreases.

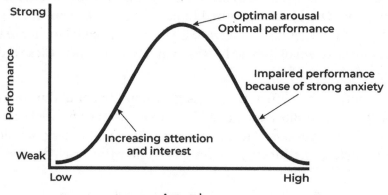

Figure 16.1: the Yerkes–Dodson law
Source: Adapted by Hebb (1955) from Robert M Yerkes and John D Dodson (1908)

The level of arousal needs to be just right in order to optimise your performance, otherwise you will either be disinterested (not enough arousal) or stressed (too much arousal).

If you find yourself sitting down to your work, and your mind is elsewhere or overwhelmed by the task at hand, there are things you can do to get your headspace right.

See the trees from the forest

It can be easy to become overwhelmed by all of the things you need to do at the detriment of doing anything at all. A useful way around this is to break those things down into manageable units. Write down all of those units, prioritise them and then focus on one at a time.

For example, launching a Google Ads campaign for a new product may sound like a lot of work and has the potential to overwhelm.

A simple breakdown of tasks may show the following, which taken one at a time (all we can actually do, by the way), helps us beat overwhelm and change our relationship with big projects.

Step 1: Research your target audience

Step 2: Research the target keywords

Step 3: Define your goals

Step 4: Create targeted landing pages

Step 5: Define your ad copy

Step 6: Determine your budget

Step 7: Test, learn and adapt.

There's no point thinking about steps 2, 3 and 4 until you are done with step 1 and have freed up the mental and physical capacity to do so.

To-do list

While the concept of to-do lists is not new, *when* you choose to write down or capture your list is important. Do you wait until you've sat down at your desk in the morning to figure out what it is you'll be working on during the day ahead? Or do you just wing it? To hit the ground running in the morning, write your to-do list at the end of the previous day. This way, your subconscious gets to work preparing for the day ahead, and you make a running start in the morning.

It also helps prevent you from spending the first 30 minutes of the day 'warming up' by reading all of the news clippings related to your company, or checking in on your Twitter feed.

Journalling

If you're stressed or suffering from a case of anxiety, journalling can help you gain control of your emotions and improve your mental health.

By writing down what's on your mind, you're transferring it onto the page. This frees up mental space to focus on your work. By transferring thoughts onto the page, you can identify the cognitive distortions or biases (see 'Negativity bias' below) that are plaguing the way you think.

I tend to journal every night before I go to sleep. This helps me fall asleep because I get things out of my head and onto paper.

Cognitive distortions 101: all-or-nothing thinking

Most things aren't black and white, or absolute. People who think in extremes and use words like 'nothing' and 'always' are all-or-nothing thinkers.

'I can never catch a break!'

'I just don't see how it will work!'

'I have too much work to do!'

'You never listen to me!'

Seeing the world through this lens makes problems out to be much bigger than they actually are.

Negativity bias

Those who tend towards mental filtering may gloss over positive events and amplify the negative ones. They might choose to focus on the one thing that went wrong instead of the ten things that went right.

An Ohio State University study, led by John Cacioppo, found that when people are shown a negative picture (a mutilated face or a dead cat), the brain demonstrates a much greater surge in electrical activity than when shown a positive picture (a Ferrari or a pizza).

Thanks to evolutionary programming, our brains are more sensitive to negative information.

This is why most media outlets focus overwhelmingly on negative news (9:1 of news stories lean negative to capture our attention. Knowing that a plane landed successfully is not news, but a plane nosediving into the middle of the Indian Ocean, killing all 450 people on board? Newsworthy).

Knowing this simple fact can help you to catch how your thoughts are colouring your perspective of life.

Practising gratitude regularly for all of the things that have gone right for you, be they great or small, can help to keep things in perspective. The media would like to have you believe that we are living in the worst times ever. Compared to when, exactly? As cognitive psychologist Steven Pinker, Swedish physician Hans Rosling and others have noted, we are, by far, living in the best times ever.

Jumping to conclusions

Two of the biggest traps that people fall into, that ultimately waste their time and energy, are analysis paralysis and jumping to conclusions.

We tend to make decisions based on assumptions that are untested and, in a world of infinite possibilities and increasing uncertainty, almost certainly not entirely true. This is why most startups and business ventures fail, taking products to market based on flawed assumptions about the underlying business model — assumptions around who will buy it, how much are they willing to pay, how big the problem is, which marketing channel will raise awareness, and so on.

Many of us can probably relate to the job recruiter or sales prospect who doesn't get back to us within a couple of days of our last correspondence. Our mind begins to race, and we conclude that the deal or job offer is dead. Then, as if by some kind of miracle, our phone rings and they'd like to proceed. Up until then, our mind was coloured by nothing but the worst possible outcome, based on nothing but an assumption. This tendency becomes more destructive when it comes to our romantic relationships, especially if we verbalise what we're assuming to our partners.

Emotional reasoning

As David Burns put it in *Feeling Good: The New Mood Therapy,* we can fall victim to ignoring facts when drawing conclusions, and rationalise our way to faulty conclusions. 'I'm feeling completely overwhelmed, so my problems must be beyond my ability to solve them' or 'I'm angry with you; you must be in the wrong here' are both examples Burns puts forward. It's when we act on faulty reasoning that we create even bigger problems for ourselves.

'Should' statements

If you find yourself saying 'should' a lot, chances are you're subscribing to rigid rules about how the world should work. As such, you're putting a lot of undue pressure on yourself to behave a certain way. For example, 'people should work late', 'people should get up at 5 am to go to the gym', 'this application should work seamlessly'. You need to see the flexibility in circumstances to overcome this.

Not everything is a should. Things are circumstantial.

Labelling and mislabelling

When we label people, we essentially paint a one-dimensional view of them, which prevents us from seeing them as they truly are. It is a shortcut to making ourselves feel good and negating the other person, without having to do any work on understanding them and learning how to best work with them.

It speaks to a lack of empathy or what I like to call 'other-awareness'.

We often fall victim to the fundamental attribution error. This cognitive bias suggests we unduly emphasise someone's character for their failings, and over-emphasise our circumstances for our own failings. We are quick to categorise and write people off as the 'bad guys' because it helps us to feel morally righteous and make sense of our world. But the world, and its people, are not black and white.

People's behaviour is rarely monocausal. There are usually a multitude of reasons converging to pre-empt a behaviour, good and bad.

Other-awareness

Self-awareness without other-awareness can only do so much for someone in a world where we need to collaborate with other people.

To best navigate the complexities of human relationships, we must develop other-awareness. By doing so, we gain an appreciation for the circumstances that shape someone else's decisions and behaviours. This makes us more empathetic and empowers us to tailor our responses and behaviour accordingly. That is, of course, if want to develop and maintain healthy relationships and optimise outcomes.

The failings of the human mind to incorporate other-awareness into how we navigate the world was demonstrated beautifully in the most unlikely of places: *The Karate Kid*-inspired *Cobra Kai* television series.

Fans of *The Karate Kid*, the iconic 1984 feature film, will remember Daniel LaRusso (Ralph Macchio) as the skinny Italian kid from Newark, New Jersey, who moved all the way to Reseda, Los Angeles. There, he was subject to constant bullying and violent attacks from local karate champion, and apparent rich kid, Johnny Lawrence (William Zabka) and his buddies from the notorious — yet ever so cool — Cobra Kai dojo.

Everybody who watched *The Karate Kid* growing up remembers gloriously raising a fist to the air the first time they watched LaRusso deliver the match-winning crane kick to Lawrence's face. This earned him the adulation of the crowd, the respect of his mentor, Mr Miyagi, and the devotion of his girl, Ali Mills.

From the perspective of the one-eyed onlooker, justice had been served. But the story looks a little different when you summon a little other-awareness.

The *Cobra Kai* television series picks up the lives of both Lawrence and LaRusso a good 35 years later.

In it, we learn that Lawrence, while he may have come across as a privileged bully, wasn't the one-dimensional character we thought he was.

The internet is full of 'Daniel is the Real Bully' memes, which observe that:

- Lawrence grew up with an abusive, neglectful stepfather.
- He sought out a father figure in the guise of his dojo's sensei, the Vietnam veteran John Kreese, instilling in a young Lawrence values like 'strike hard, strike first, no mercy'.
- LaRusso moved to town and quickly became a thorn in Lawrence's side, making moves on, and ultimately stealing, his girlfriend Ali away.
- LaRusso continued to antagonise Lawrence; during a school dance he went as far as threading a hose over a toilet cubicle to drench Lawrence — who was essentially minding his own business rolling a joint — in water.
- In many ways, LaRusso came across as the hot-tempered, arrogant trouble maker, and Lawrence was merely responding to his antagonisms.

Knowing all of this, we begin to develop a certain empathy for Lawrence's attitude and behaviour, and why he was the way he was in *The Karate Kid*. The entire *Cobra Kai* series revolves around his redemption arc and ultimately leaves the viewer rooting not for the 'balance'-seeking LaRusso (who displays anything but during the series), but the blonde-haired Lawrence.

In fact, I went full 180 and found myself repping *Cobra Kai* at a recent keynote that I gave.

We also observe that with new experiences, Lawrence's character also begins to change for the better.

It's funny, and a little scary, how our perceptions of other people, and our behaviours towards them, can shift so dramatically once we apply a little other-awareness, or conversely and perhaps more commonly, when we apply none at all.

Where might you be foregoing 'other-awareness' in your personal or professional relationships, and what might a perspective shift do for the strength of or outcomes of those relationships?

Taking things personally

In *The Four Agreements*, another of Don Miguel Ruiz's agreements, 'Don't take anything personally', points to people's tendency to blame themselves for the actions of others or for becoming overly reactive and emotional to what other people say or do.

> Nothing other people do is because of you. It is because of themselves. All people live in their own dream, in their own mind...When we take something personally, we make the assumption that they know what is in our world.

Ruiz goes on to say that if we take things personally, it makes us easy targets, and instead of going about our business with clarity and intent, we can live out our days feeling resentment and anger. As Nelson Mandela — somebody who had every reason to take things personally and resent — said, 'resentment is like drinking poison and then hoping it will kill your enemies'.

Meditation

The benefits of meditation are wide-ranging:

- reducing ageing
- reducing stress
- increasing attention spans
- improving immunity
- improving metabolism
- improving brain function
- building better relationships
- increasing your appreciation of life
- helping you get a good night's rest.

Don't overthink it. At the very least, taking just five minutes in the morning, three times a week, to focus on your breathing and merely notice thoughts come and go, can go a long way to changing your general disposition and outlook on the day ahead.

Heavy metal meditation ... metaltation?

Every now and again, I like to blast some heavy metal tunes by the likes of Slayer or Sepultura through my headphones. Why on earth would I do that? Well, like me, you probably don't live in the serenity of a tree-covered hillside — you're far more likely to be an urban dweller, or close to it. The city and its surrounds are chaotic, much like life. If you can find inner peace and focus on your breath in the middle of Sepultura's *Chaos A.D.*, you're sure to find it in the chaos of life. It's not about finding peace in peace, but finding peace in the chaos.

CALL TO ACTION

1. Write your to-do list for the next day at the end of each day.

2. Journal for five minutes at least three times a week to declutter your mind, or as my friend Matt Belair says, 'silence the teleprompter of your mind'.

3. Become more aware of cognitive biases and do your best to interject and be more proactive about how you choose to respond.

4. Be other-aware, not just self-aware.

5. Try meditating for five minutes, three times a week. Focus on your breathing—nothing fancy. Each time you notice your mind wander, just bring it back to your breathing. Slayer tunes optional.

CHAPTER 17

Sick and tired of feeling sick and tired?

We all know the feeling. We return to our desks after a boozy or carby lunch, inevitably feeling sluggish and a shadow of our usual selves for the rest of the afternoon. It's likely that the quantity and quality of work we'll churn out will suffer big time.

For those of us who enjoy the occasional drink and have on one or more occasions summoned our inner Mötley Crüe the night before a day at the office, we know what it's like to sit at our desks hungover the next morning. We're fatigued, weak, lethargic and we're not getting any work done.

But here's the thing: even without that drink the night before, most of us are heading to the office in physical states that aren't far removed from that of a food coma or a hangover.

We're underslept.

Almost one-third of Americans, and one in three Australians, get fewer than six hours' sleep a night, despite the National Sleep

Foundation recommending seven to nine hours for adults aged 18 to 64.

We're undernourished.

More than half the calories consumed by Americans come from ultra-processed foods, reflecting poor dietary choices. Down under, one-third of a typical Australian's energy intake comes from junk foods — discretionary foods such as ice-cream, chips and biscuits.

We're unfit.

Seventy-one per cent of America's youth, aged 17 to 24, would not qualify for military service. This reflects a doubling in the rate of diabetes since 1980, while about two-thirds of the United States, the UK and Australia's inhabitants are overweight or obese.

When it comes to our work, being underslept, undernourished and unfit renders us unable to truly concentrate. It takes over our memory and decision making; it makes us moody and more inclined to jeopardise relationships. It leaves us feeling lethargic, and ultimately a mere shadow of who we would otherwise be.

So what do we do? We drown ourselves in coffee and supplements that we think will offset all of the damage we're doing to our bodies and minds. But unless the fundamentals are in place, we're simply icing a non-existent cake.

Sick days are costing the Australian economy $30 billion per year, about 62 per cent of which ($18.6 billion) are taken for legitimate reasons. They are costing the United States economy US$576 billion.

How many legitimate sick days have you taken in the past year? How often have you felt unwell? How has this affected your productivity, not just when you were away from work but during the onset and recovery from illness while in the office?

I've come to realise that the fundamentals of good health and life can be broken down into eight parts, as illustrated in figure 17.1.

Figure 17.1: the eight slices of life

Purpose, freedom, mindset and sleep are foundational, and are the layer upon which nutrition, movement, growth and engaging in your community rest. If you're wondering where sex fits, it would have to be at the intersection of community (relationships) and movement, although I did think about giving sex an entire piece of the pie!

We'll hone in on the physiological building blocks — sleep, nutrition and movement — in this chapter.

Sleep

According to Matt Walker, professor of neuroscience and psychology at the University of California and author of *Why We Sleep: The New Science of Sleep and Dreams*, there are numerous reasons why people need to be getting eight hours of sleep a night. Several stand out as being of the utmost importance to entrepreneurs and leaders of teams.

Sleeping enriches a diversity of functions related to learning, memory, creativity, decision making and emotional regulation. So basically, all the important stuff your brain does.

Sadly, two-thirds of adults throughout developed nations fail to obtain the recommended eight hours of nightly sleep (the odds say you're one of them). Utterances like 'I can perform well on six hours a night', and 'eight hours is a pipe-dream' are common.

And I get it. I said the same thing for almost 10 years, willing myself out of bed at 5 am for an early-morning workout, after having slept somewhere between six and seven hours. I'd judge people who slept until 7 am and write them off as lazy and undisciplined. During my twenties and early thirties, I'd think nothing of waking up at 9 am on a Saturday morning after having gone to bed, drunk, at 5 am.

I'd venture out for a 10-kilometre run, thinking it was the best way to recover, and boast about it later. I couldn't fathom how my fellow revellers would sleep right on through to mid-afternoon.

However, the science suggests that routinely sleeping fewer than six or seven hours a night demolishes your immune system and more than doubles your risk of cancer. And the thing about thinking six hours is enough is that you don't know you're sleep deprived when you're sleep deprived.

On the creativity front, Thomas Edison would famously nap at his desk with two steel balls in both hands when challenged by a daunting problem. On the floor, directly below his closed hands, he placed metal saucers. As he entered what's known as 'the transitional state between wakefulness and sleep', Edison would drop the steel balls onto the saucer, effectively waking him up. He'd then furiously write down anything he was thinking about just before he was awoken by the loud crash.

EIGHT THINGS YOU CAN DO TO GET A BETTER NIGHT'S SLEEP

1. Set your bedroom temperature at 18 degrees Celsius/ 64 degrees Fahrenheit.

2. Don't look at devices or blue light (smartphones, tablets, laptops) within an hour of bed and keep light to an absolute minimum. A bedside lamp is 20–80 lux and a living room is 200 lux, suppressing melatonin by 50 per cent. Even 8–10 lux delays melatonin release, making it

harder for you to fall asleep. If you must, wear blue-light suppressing glasses or 'blue blockers'.

3. Journal: get thoughts out of your head and onto paper.

4. Have a hot bath, a hot shower or a sauna before you hit the hay. Doing so will make it easier to fall asleep as your body begins its cooling down process.

5. Don't drink alcohol before bed (you might be able to fall asleep on a glass of red or a glass of whiskey, but the quality of that sleep will be more akin to a sedated sleep than a natural one, and you're more likely to wake up in the middle of the night as the alcohol wears off).

6. Don't eat a large meal just before bed.

7. Down a magnesium supplement before bed. Magnesium, dubbed by many the original chill pill, is an old home remedy for all that ails you. In 1968, a research paper by Warren Wacker and Alfred Parisi found that magnesium deficiency could cause depression, behavioural disturbances, headaches, muscle cramps, seizures, ataxia, psychosis and irritability—all reversible with magnesium repletion. And it's great for calming you down for a good night's rest.

8. Don't consume engaging content or media just before bed.

... actually, there are nine:

9. Have more sex (more on this shortly!).

Coffee

Being born and raised in Melbourne, arguably the world's coffee capital, there are few simple pleasures I enjoy more than a trip to my local café to pick up a strong latte or an Ethiopian roast filter coffee. Despite its critics, coffee offers numerous health benefits: it boosts your metabolism; improves circulation, alertness and energy; and even reduces your risk of some cancers and heart disease. Now, with every yin, there's usually a yang.

Coffee's half-life — the time taken for the body to eliminate one-half of the caffeine consumed — is five to six hours. If you enjoy a coffee at 3 pm, you've still got about half of it in your system come 9 pm. While you might not make the connection between an afternoon coffee and insomnia, there is a strong case to be made for it. Even if you *do* manage to fall asleep, the quality of that sleep will suffer. In both cases, you will likely wake up with all of the symptoms of sleep deprivation.

A NASA study from 1995 demonstrates how toxic caffeine is for the brain. Researchers exposed spiders to the toxic substances caffeine, marijuana, Benzedrine and chloral hydrate, and then observed the quality of webs they would weave. The greater the toxicity, the more sides of a web a spider fails to complete (see figure 17.2).

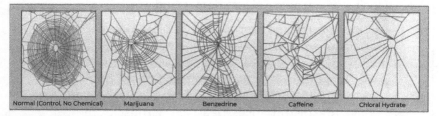

Figure 17.2: the effect of toxicity on a spider weaving a web
Source: NASA

While I still enjoy my morning coffee nowadays, given that I get to sleep at about 10 pm most weeknights, I tend to shut the gates on caffeine consumption at midday, so as not to affect the quality of my sleep.

Nutrition

Industrialisation has been one of the great wonders of humanity and propelled us to new heights. It gave us, among other things, running water, electricity, lighting, vaccinations, the automobile, air travel and, apparently, more food than we can handle. Sadly, most of this food is processed junk that serves to keep the margins of big food as big as our waistlines.

Here's a sobering statistic—40 per cent of Americans and 30 per cent of Australians are now obese.

So many financially successful people will put nothing but premium unleaded fuel in their luxury vehicles, but won't think twice about starting their day with a deep fried hash brown or a large bowl of sugar — and that's just how they *start* their day.

There's little point exercising each day if you're just going to stuff your face with simple carbs such as sugars and starch, food prepared in toxic vegetable oils, and packaged goods that list more chemicals than natural ingredients on their label.

So what should you eat to support a productive lifestyle?

Good fats, clean proteins, small servings of low-GI carbs and fermented foods (for your gut) are the premium unleaded fuel for the productive go-getter.

While those who are dogmatic about nutrition may tell you that you need to get 80 per cent of your calories from fat, or all of your calories from plants, or all of your calories from 'paleo' foods or even all of your calories from meat, the reality is that each one of us is different, with our own unique biophysiology and our own unique lifestyles, and that we should try different things to see what works for us.

If you want a little more actionable advice, here are author Michael Pollan's '7 Rules for Eating' in a nutshell:

1. Don't eat anything that wouldn't have existed when your great-grandparents were alive.
2. Don't eat anything that contains more than five ingredients or anything that you can't pronounce.
3. Shop in the outer parts of the store, where the fresh foods are usually found.
4. Only eat food that will rot if you don't eat it.
5. Stop eating before you feel full.
6. Have regular meals, with your family members — around a table, not in front of the TV.
7. Don't buy food at the petrol station because you're likely to eat it in the car.

As Pollan says, 'Eat food, not too much, mostly plants.'

Balance in blue

Journalist Dan Buettner, in partnership with *National Geographic* magazine, has identified five 'blue zones': places in the world where people live longer and healthier lives than anywhere else on earth. Several such zones exist, and in each of these places, living to 90 or even 100 is common, comparing favourably to the 79-year life expectancy in the United States.

The five blue zones are:

- Sardinia, Italy
- Okinawa, Japan
- Loma Linda, California
- Nicoya Peninsula, Costa Rica
- Ikaria, Greece.

Not only do people in these blue zones live longer, but they also have long health spans — they're free from debilitating diseases for the vast majority of their lives.

I spoke with Kale Brock, the filmmaker behind *The Longevity Film*, who visited Ikaria, Okinawa and Loma Linda to better understand their lifestyles and what predisposed these people to long, healthy lives. He found that they enjoyed meaningful work, strong relationships, lifestyles prone to movement, and diets high in plants, good fats and clean proteins. He also found that they weren't averse to smoking a cigarette during a break or having a glass of red wine with dinner. The difference is in the balance.

Brock says we tend to oscillate between extremes in the west:

We sit at our desks for ten or so hours, then smash ourselves in the gym for 45 minutes, we binge drink. You can sit alone in the corner drinking a green smoothie, but your friends sitting at the bar having a beer might actually be healthier than you are at that given time because they're conversing with each other.

In short, while I'm not endorsing smoking, or drinking, optimal health isn't just about exercise and nutrition, but so much of it has to do with meaningful work, meaningful relationships and balance (which we've touched on already).

I might enjoy a gelato with a friend at Melbourne's famous Messina gelateria, but I won't do this every single day. When it comes to nutrition, it comes down to a golden rule I like to call 'Don't be a dickhead'.

Nutrition and the gut

Beneficial microbes such as lactobacilli or bifidobacteria — delivered by fermented foods such as yogurts, sauerkraut and kimchi, or in probiotic capsules — may improve the diversity of the gut microbiome ecosystem.

Broad-spectrum antibiotics, for example, reduce the populations of gamma aminobutyric acid (GABA)-producing bacteria, which can affect our focus.

Studies suggest heightened GABA can help us regulate anxiety and fear, and therefore create the space for focus.

Mediators of our stress systems such as the stress hormone norepinephrine, can profoundly alter gut microbial behaviour, making them more aggressive and dangerous.

Fasting and focus

Intermittent fasting — or IF — refers to cycling between periods of fasting and non-fasting. Popular forms of IF involve fasting for 16 hours a day and only eating during the other eight hours. Lucas Aoun of Ergogenic Health puts it like this:

> IF is one of the most accessible health hacks that virtually anyone can implement into their lifestyle. Unlike health supplements, fasting costs you nothing ... it actually saves you money!

IF has been shown to release growth hormone (GH), which has anti-ageing properties, stimulates fat loss and supports muscle growth.

Of importance, IF stimulates autophagy, which is a bodily process that recycles damaged cells and cleans up cellular waste. Ben Greenfield, human guinea-pig and founder of holistic health company Kion, says that fasting for as little as 12 hours can have benefits insofar as this cellular cleanup is concerned.

Autophagy helps to regenerate and detoxify the body. It can help to reduce inflammation and increase neuroplasticity and cognitive functions.

Ancient Greek philosophers were known to fast to improve their mental agility.

If food was scarce for a caveman during the winter months, cognitive function was actually elevated, making it possible to hunt for food.

I tend to engage in 14- to 16-hour daily fasts, and reserve my deep thinking work for the morning when I'm in a fasted state and find myself with a higher level of focus and cognition.

Other benefits of fasting include lower blood glucose and insulin levels, a reduced risk of various types of cancer, a decrease in cardiovascular disease risk, increased HDL cholesterol and lowered LDL cholesterol.

Nootropics and cognitive enhancers

Smart drugs, known in Silicon Valley as 'nootropics', are cognitive enhancers that support focus, memory, creativity and motivation. Popular products worth checking out include Teelixir's Lion's Mane, Onnit's Alpha Brain, Four Sigmatic's Mushroom Coffee, Bulletproof Coffee's Brain Octane and Ergogenic Health's BrainX (full disclosure: I'm an investor in the latter).

The lion's mane mushroom alone has been found to have numerous physiological benefits, apart from boosting cognitive performance, including:

- controlling inflammation and oxidation
- controlling immune function
- controlling anxiety and depression
- controlling blood-sugar levels.

However, supplements like these are the icing on the cake, and will do little for someone who is underslept, undernourished and unfit.

Movement

As we established early in this book, at the dawn of the 20th century, 40 per cent of Americans worked in agriculture, with the vast majority of the rest in coal mines and on factory floors. Prior to that, humanity evolved from being hunter-gatherers to—for about 10 000 years or so, leading up to the Industrial Revolution—farmers or soldiers. For the vast majority of humanity's time on this earth, we have spent a lot of our day being physically active.

Yet, more and more we find ourselves sitting down at our desks, staring at LED screens for eight to ten hours a day, before sitting down on our couches in the evenings, staring at an LED screen for a few hours more—at least, that's what life looks like for a disturbingly large percentage of today's population.

So while we've found less painful and more sedentary ways to generate wealth than lugging carts full of coal through air-deprived tunnels, it has come at a cost not only to our waistlines, but also to our emotional wellbeing and physical health.

Movement, not necessarily a gym session—in fact outdoors is preferable—has been shown to decrease anxiety and ward off depression, memory loss and more.

So what happens when you move? Well, your caveman brain recognises movement as a moment of stress. It thinks you're fighting an enemy, or fleeing, and as such, it releases BDNF (brain-derived neurotrophic factor). This ultimately acts as a reset switch, which is why we feel happier after exercising or going for a walk.

As researchers from the University of Illinois found, the brain lights up like a Christmas tree after a short walk (see figure 17.3, overleaf). I love to quote Seneca because so much of his writings were astonishingly validated by science two millennia later. The philosopher said, 'we must go for walks out of doors, so that the mind can be strengthened and invigorated by a clear sky and plenty of fresh air.'

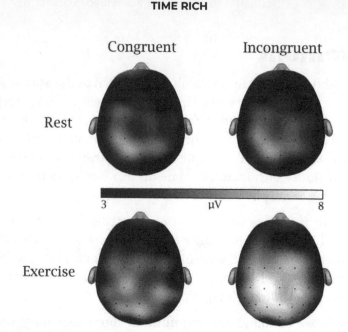

Figure 17.3: brain activity after walking
Source: Hillman, C, Pontifex, M, Raine, L, Castelli, D, Hall, E and
Kramer, A. (2009). The effect of acute treadmill walking on
cognitive control and academic achievement in preadolescent
children. *Neuroscience*, 159(3), pp. 1044–1054.

You don't necessarily need to smash yourself in the gym. The key is to
incorporate more *movement* into your entire day: go for a lunchtime
walk, take the stairs, have more walking or standing-up meetings,
walk to the train station or park a little further from the office than
you normally do. All of these things add up—and they're likely to be,
on aggregate, much better for you than being sedentary all day long
and going for a 30-minute workout after work.

Outdoors

It's one thing to move, but where you choose to move also affects your
physiology, and ultimately, how you feel.

Sunlight

Exposure to sunlight in the morning elevates mood by boosting
serotonin levels in our body, which makes us perform better when
we get down to work. Author of *Stress-Proof* Dr Mithu Storoni also

found that morning sunlight improves our sleep — 'The brighter your daylight exposure, the more melatonin you produce at night' — again helping us to perform better when we're at work. A 2017 study in the *Journal of Human Resources* found that students who get more sunlight perform better in tests.

Sun exposure can even aid weight loss, with one study revealing that basking in morning sunshine for just 20 to 30 minutes can reduce body fat and lower your BMI (body mass index).

In fact, legendary music producer Rick Rubin credits waking up early and getting 20 minutes of exposure to sunlight as one of the key reasons behind his losing 130 pounds.

Unfortunately, if your only exposure to morning sunlight is through the glass of your windshield, then the effects are nulled as the glass absorbs about 97 per cent of the sun rays.

Of course, you should apply common sense when it comes to sunlight, and not overdo it, as the effects of too much exposure to nasty UV rays are well documented.

Grounding

You might have noticed an upswing in the number of people walking around your neighbourhood barefoot, and wondered whether the apparent rise in hipsters will conflate with an increase in property values. But aside from an increase in property prices, these barefooted folks are also enjoying an improvement in mood, blood circulation and energy. Turns out they're not just making a statement; they're engaging in something that has become known as 'grounding', or 'earthing' — that is, to walk around outside barefoot.

A 20-year body of research has found that the human body demonstrates positive physiological responses to grounding, benefitting our mood, sleep, blood circulation and energy while decreasing bodily inflammation and free radicals in the body.

At its core, grounding helps us connect to the earth's subtle negative electrical charge, which, when absorbed, acts like an antioxidant and can help to create a stable, internal, bioelectrical environment for the normal functioning of the body, according to a report in the *Journal of Environmental and Public Health*. While rubber-soled shoes and sneakers insulate us from lightning that strikes the ground, they also insulate us from the earth's electromagnetic current.

Ultimately though, an experience that I hope everybody reading this can relate to is walking barefoot at the beach. We tend to walk away with a sunnier disposition, and while time with friends in the sun no doubt lifts our spirits, grounding, it turns out, is also playing a role.

Of course, there's no need to walk around your neighbourhood barefoot like a relic of Woodstock; try it in parks, nature reserves and at the beach, or even in your backyard if you have one.

Forest bathing

Finally, when it comes to the outdoors, the benefits of a walk in nature—or 'forest bathing', as it has come to be known—has been linked to more relaxation, less stress and more insights with which to navigate our work and personal lives.

I tend to try and get out for a two-hour hike in the forest at least once a month, and go for daily walks in a local park, which does wonders for my sense of emotional wellbeing. In fact, 94 per cent of adults surveyed said that 20 minutes in a park boosted feelings of wellbeing, while the practice decreased cortisol levels and lowered depression levels in adults.

Struggling to find time outdoors? Have a meeting—if you must have a meeting—while walking outside.

Sitting all day

We're all aware that sitting all day is damaging our bodies in various ways. Standing lowers your risk of weight gain and obesity, lowers blood sugar levels, lowers your risk of heart disease, reduces back pain, improves mood and energy levels, boosts productivity and focus, and ultimately helps you live longer.

One US study found that reducing sitting time to three hours a day would raise the average American's life expectancy by two years.

In addition, standing for a couple of hours each afternoon burns more than 150 calories, accounting for almost 1000 calories a week, equivalent to one kilogram lost every seven weeks. According to the UK's *Daily Mail*, getting up from your desk for just two minutes every half an hour can slash your risk of diabetes.

Consider investing in a standing desk, which can be purchased for a few hundred dollars from Ergotron or Kogan. Or, if you're feeling really game, people such as XPRIZE founder Peter Diamandis and author Gretchen Rubin swear by the treadmill desk.

However, before you spend all day standing, consider a 2017 study by Curtin University which found that 'prolonged standing may have health and productivity impacts'. After working on computers at standing desks for two hours, study participants reported 'discomfort', 'muscle fatigue' and 'lower limb swelling'.

Alex Hutchinson, author of *Endure*, and *Runner's World* contributor, says that standing all day is twice as bad as sitting for your heart...which runs counter to 'sitting is the new smoking'.

Instead, we should walk more. People who walk for just two minutes every hour, have a 33 per cent lower risk of premature death than sedentary peers, according to a 2015 study published in the *Clinical Journal of the American Society of Nephrology*.

Exercise

As we've already established, incorporating movement into your entire day is the goal. But that doesn't mean you should cancel your gym membership, as there are numerous benefits that come from specific types of exercises that a walk won't offer. For example, strength training protects bone health and muscle mass, which are critical to maintaining a high quality of life and mobility as we age. The average person loses about 3 to 5 per cent of lean muscle mass per year once they turn 30, and strength training helps to combat this erosion.

Different activities offer different benefits — whether they be physiological or emotional. Yoga, Pilates, gymnastics, strength training, powerlifting, swimming, running, cycling, martial arts, surfing, soccer, basketball, rock climbing, skateboarding, primal movements...the world is your gym. Do what you enjoy, and what makes a difference to your experience and quality of life.

Even a 15-minute bodyweight routine outdoors can go a long way.

Tom Corley, author of *Rich Habits*, spent five years studying 233 rich people and 128 poor people. He found that most rich people partake in at least a 30-minute daily exercise routine.

I'm an early bird, so I tend to get a 30-minute workout in first thing in the morning. It's a form of priming and it not only puts me in a good mood, and focuses my energy, but it also starts my day overcoming that little voice in my head that never relents to urge me to hit snooze.

Cold showers

According to Lucas Aoun, cold showers have numerous proven physiological benefits, such as reducing inflammation, enhancing immunity and supporting fat loss. From a performance perspective, cold showers release dopamine and norepinephrine, which as we learned earlier, promote feelings of wellbeing, energy and confidence.

This is probably why motivational guru Tony Robbins likes to start his days with a cold plunge into a 57-degree Fahrenheit pool of water — equivalent to 14 degrees Celsius. To put that into perspective, the average temperature in Melbourne's Port Phillip Bay is 15 degrees Celsius in winter and the water temperature in San Diego's share of the Pacific Ocean during the winter is basically equivalent to that of Tony Robbins' plunge pool.

Aside from that, starting your day with a cold shower — especially in the dead of winter — is a great way to build adversity into your day, sharpen your discipline and set yourself up to be ready for anything.

Let's talk about sex

Ever since Salt-N-Pepa released their hit single in 1990, sex has become less a stigma and more a widely accepted, and widely enjoyed, staple of life.

But it's more than just something that feels good; having regular sex has numerous neurological benefits that ultimately serve to help us enjoy life more and perform at a higher level.

Firstly, sex (and to a degree, cuddling) releases those powerful neurochemicals we introduced earlier — serotonin, dopamine and endorphins as well as oxytocin (the social bonding hormone) — leaving us feeling confident and happy.

Not only that, but sex makes it easier to get a good night's rest. A powerful orgasm to a male is equal to a 2-3 mg shot of Valium.

Regular sex also helps to keep oestrogen and testosterone levels in balance — without which a host of problems emerge, and without which our susceptibility to heart disease increases.

Finally, males who ejaculate at least 21 times a month have a lower risk of developing prostate cancer.

So there you have it — science-backed reasons for why you should be having more sex, just in case you needed to convince your partner!

CALL TO ACTION

1. Optimise your sleep (eight hours should be the goal).
2. Watch your coffee intake, and in particular, when you drink it.
3. Eat well most of the time.
4. Take a daily probiotic or eat probiotic-rich fermented foods like yogurt.
5. Give fasting a go. Start with a once-a-week, 12-hour fast and work your way up.
6. Incorporate more sunlight, preferably in the morning, into your day.
7. Incorporate more movement into your entire day, preferably outdoors.
8. Have regular sex.
9. Enjoy balance.

CHAPTER 18
Productivity tips and tricks

Thomas Edison was responsible for 1093 patents and inventions that continue to impact our lives today, from the electric generator and electric pen, to the fuel cell, storage battery and telephone transmitter.

Edison is considered by many to be the father of the to-do list, something productivity gurus today swear by (see an example in figure 18.1).

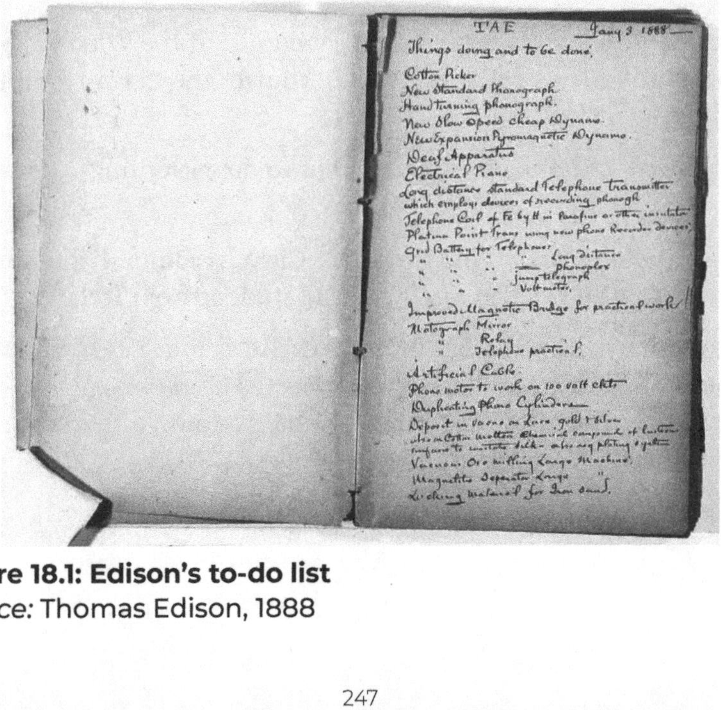

Figure 18.1: Edison's to-do list
Source: Thomas Edison, 1888

I've found that high performers all have some kind of ritual or routine they partake in, in order to get the most out of every day.

In this chapter, I'll introduce some productivity tools and techniques that haven't featured elsewhere in this book, but that would be remiss of me not to include.

The Pomodoro Technique

Francesco Cirillo developed the popular Pomodoro Technique in the late 1980s. It essentially involves breaking work down into 25 minute intervals, separated by five-minute breaks.

After four rounds, take a long break of between 15 and 30 minutes, before repeating the cycle.

While I'm not a staunch advocate or practitioner of the Pomodoro Technique, many swear by it. I prefer to get into flow and then work until I hit a wall, which is usually about an hour, at which point, I need to get up, stretch, go for a 10-minute walk, and then get back to it.

Task bundling

Katherine Milkman, a behavioural economist at the Wharton School of the University of Pennsylvania, coined the term 'temptation bundling'.

It refers to bundling things you *want* to do with things you *need* to do, to help you build positive habits.

In his book *Atomic Habits*, James Clear recounted the story of Ronan Byrne, an electrical engineering student from Ireland.

Byrne enjoyed Netflix but didn't exercise as much as he should. To engineer his way around this, he connected a stationary bike to his computer, and wrote a program that would allow Netflix to run only if he was cycling at a certain speed.

He was combining something he wanted to do—watch Netflix—with something he needed to do—exercise.

This is not only a great way to build habits, but a fantastic way to save time, and can extend to all sorts of activities.

Let's say my physiotherapist asked me to incorporate 30 minutes of mobility training into my day, three times a week. I could combine this with watching a documentary on YouTube, or even taking a call on speaker.

Want to learn more about astrophysics but between work and family, you don't have the time? You could listen to Neil deGrasse Tyson's podcast while shopping for groceries or commuting.

You might be saying, 'but I thought we weren't capable of multitasking, Steve?', and you'd be right. However, task bundling is different because we're not switching between work tasks and suffering a switching penalty. We're just bundling, or stacking, non-work tasks in order to free up more time for either work or play.

Nevertheless, when it comes to work, you can benefit from bundling tasks. For example, if I'm waiting for my designer to come back to me with our new set of Facebook ad images, I *could* wait until they get back to me to set up the ad campaign, or I could layer this task. What this means is that while I wait for the designs, I'll set up the ad campaign, and simply plug in the designs when I receive them. Done properly, this means my team and I can achieve much more over the course of the year than we otherwise would if we were always waiting for dependent tasks to be completed before we started on the next task.

Task bundling is nothing new to project management professionals who know their way around a good old fashioned Gantt chart. It might sound like common sense, but it's something that doesn't come naturally to so many entrepreneurs and executives I've worked with, and when called out it triggers an 'aha' moment, much to my surprise.

Think multi-benefit, not mono-benefit

Certain types of tasks are rich in benefits — what I call multi-benefit.

Surfing offers the following benefits:

- cardiovascular fitness
- muscular strength
- time in the outdoors and nature
- emotional regulation and de-stressing
- socialising (if surfing with a friend or two)
- cold and saltwater therapy
- resilience building.

If you weren't deliberately bundling, you might instead obtain these benefits by investing time in each of the following tasks:

- cycling on a stationary bike at the gym (cardio)
- lifting weights at the gym (muscular strength)
- going for a hike (the outdoors)
- going to cryotherapy (cold therapy)
- floating in a sensory deprivation tank (saltwater and emotional regulation)
- going to dinner with friends (socialising)
- attending a philosophy class (resilience).

While you might surf for an hour, the above-mentioned tasks could take you a day to complete. I'm not proposing you drop doing all of these things completely. Each have their own benefits.

By being more intentional about what you want to invest time into, and bundling, you'll find yourself with a lot more free time on your hands. This is especially true when you replace a few mono-benefit activities with one multi-benefit activity such as surfing.

Chances are you're already doing a lot of bundling unwittingly, but by being deliberate about it, you can unlock quick wins that can earn you back hours of your life.

Deliberate task bundling is as easy as:

- making a list of what you want to invest time in and develop (your fitness, your friendships, your knowledge, and so on)
- making a list of your day-to-day mono-benefit tasks
- dropping the tasks that don't serve you
- combining the remaining mono-benefit tasks
- where possible, replacing several of these tasks with a multi-benefit task.

Don't focus on the number of tasks you're getting done, but on the benefit accrued.

Do the hardest things first

With your environment and physiological and mental states set, do the hardest things first. As we've established, once you start building momentum, it's much easier to keep going.

I had the pleasure of speaking with Remi Adeleke, former Nigerian royalty, turned teenage drug dealer in the Bronx, turned Navy Seal, turned Hollywood actor (quite the story), for an episode of *Future Squared*. He spoke of his own challenges writing his autobiography, *Transformed*.

He even went as far as hiring a ghost writer to write the last four chapters, until his publisher pushed back on the idea. 'I ended up writing the last four chapters in just a month and a half — and once I got into flow, it was easy.'

We often shy away from doing things for both biological reasons, and out of fear. That shouldn't stop us from trying. And it's this very act of trying that builds momentum, gets us into flow, and helps make what moments ago seemed incredibly intimidating (like writing those last four chapters) somewhat easy in retrospect.

Don't put off the hard things for when your cognition is not at its sharpest. Take advantage. You don't bring on Michael Jordan for the last few minutes of a game—you take advantage of that asset right from the start!

STOP when you're feeling sluggish

So you've had a relatively productive day, but come 2 pm you're feeling yourself drop off. STOP what you're doing.

Take some time to reflect on how much more you can reasonably get done that day from a cognition perspective, how important and urgent the tasks you're working on are, and decide whether you will get back to it later or wrap up for the day.

If it's the former, get up and go for a walk. Give your brain some space to reset before willing it to do some more work.

Paradoxically, if you want to get more work done, try taking more—not fewer—breaks. I cringe whenever I see people eat lunch at their desk because they're 'so busy'.

The Draugiem Group installed software to track their employees' productivity. They found that the top 10 per cent of employees didn't work more hours but instead, that they took more breaks. On average, the high-performers worked for 52 minutes followed by a 17-minute break.

It's inevitable that we will experience cognitive decline as the day unfolds, so it is critical that we incorporate frequent breaks into our day, to optimise our 'pulse and pause' cycle.

CALL TO ACTION

Here are some steps you can take to navigate towards becoming time rich.

1. Create the best conditions for eight hours of sleep a night (*hint:* if you want to be able to go to bed early, then wake up early!).

2. Stand up and move more while you're at work.

3. Try intermittent fasting and the occasional cold shower and see what it does for your focus.

4. Exercise for 30 minutes at least three times a week (walking on a treadmill doesn't count).

5. Get your 10 000 steps in each day.

6. Keep junk food to a minimum, but allow yourself cheat meals (it's about eating well most of the time, not all of the time).

7. Try the Pomodoro Technique, or similar 'pulse and pause' techniques.

What now?

If you've followed the suggestions in this book, by now you should be time rich. So what will you do with all that newfound freedom?

Throughout recorded history, humanity has fought for freedom.

Whether it was Odysseus and his crew fighting for freedom from a man-eating cyclops, the people of the Balkans fighting for freedom from Ottoman rule, or Martin Luther King Jr fighting for civil liberties and true freedom for African-Americans, freedom is a fundamental human need.

In fact, the United Nations lists freedom from slavery and torture, and freedom of opinion and expression, as fundamental human rights.

When we don't have it, our being suffers. We fail to become actualised versions of ourselves. We don't even have the *opportunity* to try.

But it's not just freedom *from* things that matters.

It's also freedom *to do* things.

If you've applied the lessons put forward in this book, you will no doubt find yourself with way more free time.

What are you going to do with that free time?

On feeling guilty

Having grown up in a capitalist society, and surrounded myself with entrepreneurial people and content, I can sometimes feel a little guilty. There's so much narrative out there on #hustle culture and working hard.

When I find myself at the beach at 3 pm while the rest of the world is *seemingly* hard at work, it can invoke guilt.

But then I remind myself: I've developed systems and outsourced work, which means that while I'm at the beach, X value is being generated—the equivalent of my working 12 plus hours. Not only that, but I've already spent several hours in deep work that day, and any subsequent investment would only be in vain, and would cost me and my business pursuits in the long term.

On being bored

Think back to when you were a child. There was nothing on television. It was raining outside. You had mastered all of your video games and toys. You had read all of your books. Your friends, like you, were house stricken. And your siblings and parents had other matters to tend to.

You probably found yourself painfully bored.

According to John Eastwood and colleagues, the widely accepted psychological definition of boredom is 'the aversive experience of wanting, but being unable, to engage in satisfying activity'.

When's the last time you truly found yourself bored today?

The chances are that at the first hint of boredom or inactivity you simply reached for your phone to check out the latest tweets or stories on social media. Or perhaps you switched on Netflix to check out the latest episode of *Vikings* or the new special from Chris D'Elia (check him out, he's hilarious).

But there are numerous benefits to being bored.

There are conferences on the topic, such as the International Interdisciplinary Boredom Conference and London's The Boring Conference.

A British study found that subjects who were primed with a boring activity first, are more prolific at a subsequent creative challenge than those who dive head first into the challenge.

Boredom might be elusive in our always-on world, but that doesn't make it any less fertile when it comes to unlocking our creativity.

Being bored not only makes us more creative, but provides space for personal reflection so that we can connect with that voice inside us, better understand ourselves and better make decisions to guide our life's trajectory.

Next time you're feeling bored, resist the urge to do something, and just sit with your thoughts. You might be surprised by what you learn.

DEEP LEISURE: ARE YOU LIVING OR EXISTING?

I went snowboarding at Australia's Mount Hotham in the winter of 2019.

While I've been a long-time skateboarder and short-time surfer, I'd never been snowboarding.

Although my skating skills were *somewhat* transferable, it didn't stop my arse from hitting the white powder more than 100 times over the weekend.

But that was okay.

It just meant that I had to get up 101 times.

Every time I fell down, a little voice in my head urged me to take a break and head inside to the warmth of a café for a coffee and to chill.

And every time, I silenced that voice, got back up and kept going.

By the end of the weekend, I was nailing S-turns and even attempting 180 jumps.

(continued)

DEEP LEISURE: ARE YOU LIVING OR EXISTING? (*cont'd*)

My body was in pain on the subsequent Monday and Tuesday.

And I loved it.

The pain is a reminder that you're living.

If you're not experiencing physical or mental discomfort every now and again, you're not pushing yourself and becoming the best possible version of yourself.

If this is you, then you're not really *living*—you're existing.

If it's been a while since your muscles ached or you felt your heart beating wildly in anticipation of doing something that scares you—like giving a talk in front of 100 people—make plans to get out of your comfort zone.

Don't forget to say 'no!' to that little voice in your head urging you to quit, and keep going.

Life's too short not to!

Hiding behind the veil of work

It's easy to hide behind the veil of work to avoid confronting yourself in the real world, outside of our figurative office walls. It's easy to rationalise doing so, especially when society tends to look favourably upon and rewards people who work hard and long hours.

It's easy to hide behind the veil of work without truly working on ourselves.

Watch out for this tendency, which is plaguing people's lives the world over.

What will I say on my deathbed?

Bronnie Ware is an Australian nurse who spent several years working in palliative care, caring for patients in the last 12 weeks of their lives. She captured her observations in her book, *The Top Five Regrets of the Dying*.

In no particular order, the top five regrets she found were:

- I wish I'd had the courage to live a life true to myself, not the life others expected of me. (This was the most common regret of all.)
- I wish I hadn't worked so hard.
- I wish I'd had the courage to express my feelings.
- I wish I'd stayed in touch with my friends.
- I wish I'd let myself be happier.

As Michael Shermer said on my podcast, '"I wish I worked 80 hours a week instead of 70," said nobody on their deathbed, ever.'

Having heard elderly people echo the five regrets, I got to work on better prioritising, automating and outsourcing what we do at Collective Campus. Over time, this resulted in downward pressure on the hours we needed to work.

Suddenly, I had a lot more time to myself, and this was confronting, because it forced me to come face-to-face with the fact that I had deficiencies across various aspects of life that work ultimately shielded me from.

At this point, it was time for me to address those deficiencies. I'm by no means perfect, and am still on, and will probably always be on, the journey. We never truly arrive, and as Aristotle said, we should aim to cultivate virtues between a vice of excess and deficiency.

Who do you want to be?

It is said that there are more dead human beings than live ones; the argument being that over the course of human history over 100 billion human beings have lived, but only 7 billion are breathing today.

But I'd take that stat further.

Of the 7 billion that are breathing today, how many are truly *living*?

Ultimately, when you find yourself with a lot more free time, you have two choices:

1. reinvest that time back into your work
2. invest that time into other aspects of your character.

Take that dancing course you've always wanted to do. Become a Brazilian Jiu jitsu black belt. Learn how to surf.

Whatever your poison, it's worth reflecting on how you'll use that spare time, and do it deliberately.

Reflect on:

- what aspects of your character you want to develop
- what fills you with joy
- what you want to learn.

When I found myself with more spare time, I didn't just turn on the telly and mindlessly stuff my face with popcorn while I binge watched an entire season of *Orange Is the New Black*.

I reflected on how I wanted to invest that time so I'd get better as a person, but also find myself feeling better, with a greater sense of energy and of actually living.

What aspects of my character did I want to develop?

- be more social
- develop a better relationship with adversity
- become funnier.

What fills me with joy?

- being in nature
- movement
- deep conversations.

What did I want to learn?

- how to surf
- how to snowboard.

Based on a quick stocktake, I invested my spare time into the following:

- learning the fundamentals of standup comedy and hitting the open-mic circuit for a string of performances (some of which I would rather forget, but that were character-building nonetheless!)
- starting a podcast to connect with and converse with deep thinkers
- attending more social events to do the same
- often taking long weekends, or working from the coast so I could increase the number of hours I spend surfing exponentially and thus become a better surfer
- spending more time checking out hiking trails
- getting back into martial arts
- satisfying my creative itch to draw.

This is just scratching the surface, but by doing these things, I essentially moved closer to who I want to be, but also just felt better.

Building wealth

Automating and outsourcing many aspects of my core business and income-producing asset has given me the freedom to get my financial affairs in order.

It freed up headspace and time to invest in setting up an effective financial structure using a discretionary trust.

It freed me up to invest time looking into property, stock and bond investment opportunities.

It freed me up to look at compelling business investment and acquisition opportunities, to which I apply the fundamentals taught in this book to create financial value and wealth — wealth that again gives me the freedom *from* things and the freedom *to do* things.

But it's all at my own pace. And it's all about doing things that align with my own values, strengths and interests.

It's all about singing from *my own* songbook, not somebody else's.

Because when you spend your life singing from somebody else's songbook, you end up feeling as empty as a bass player in a tribute band.

Final thoughts

In an always-on world, overwhelm has become our default state, but it doesn't need to be.

By reflecting on what we truly value, and then applying the techniques and tools put forward in this book, we can not only find ourselves feeling a lot less overwhelmed, and in fact, feeling in total control, but also living a life in alignment with what we value and what brings us joy.

Rather than seek to numb our internal narrative through all sorts of unhealthy pursuits, applying the lessons learned in this book will provide you with the mental space and the clarity to essentially silence that narrative by rendering it baseless.

Life is too short to spend it doing something that the economy or technology will render worthless in years to come.

While I was writing this book, I published a piece on Medium on ambition, which was very well received, and I couldn't think of a better way to end this book than to reprint it here, as it ultimately closes the loop on what this book is all about: liberating you physically, cognitively, emotionally and spiritually to live your best life — in the office and outside of it.

PHILOSOPHY STOLE MY AMBITION

Like all human beings, I have insecurities.

Most of these insecurities stem from childhood.

And like most 'bad' things, in small doses, they can be good for us.

(continued)

PHILOSOPHY STOLE MY AMBITION (cont'd)

Insecurities can fuel our fire. They can drive us to seek out external validation and as a result, achieve more and become more than we would have without them.

There's little doubt that many great innovations of the past few centuries were a result of innovators looking to prove themselves.

On the flipside, peaking early can be inherently bad for us, and keep us from self-actualisation.

In my case, insecurity, societal influences, a desire to keep up with the Joneses (whoever they are) and a belief that more money and status would make me happy pushed me forward.

It drove me to secure my Master's degree in a year while working 25 hours a week. It enabled me to hustle my way into gigs at global powerhouses like EY, KPMG and Macquarie Bank, despite having gone to public schools in Melbourne's working-class western suburbs and having attended run-of-the-mill colleges.

After several years in the corporate space, my hunger hadn't faded, and I pursued entrepreneurship. This culminated in my founding several companies, one of which—unlike the others—went on to become one of Australia's fastest growing companies.

By ordinary measures of success, I guess you could say I was successful.

But...I wasn't *content*.

Searching for truth

Legend has it that one day Socrates and his student Plato were walking down the beach in deep conversation. Plato asked Socrates to tell him the truth. Long story short, Socrates dunked Plato's head into the water, only to resurface it once Plato was about to black out (some say Socrates had to revive him). When Plato asked Socrates why he did that, Socrates responded with, 'When you desire the truth like you desired air right now, then you shall have it.'

And I guess that's what I was looking for. The truth.

We seek answers to big questions when we go through difficulty. In my case, I had worked hard for almost a decade to become somebody, yet the supposed void and irritability I was confronted with forced me to seek out philosophy.

Listening to an episode of *The Tim Ferriss Show*, I stumbled upon Stoicism, and by extension, other schools and works of philosophy.

Before these ideas could save me, they had to destroy me.

These are the ideas that stole my ambition.

The man who craves more is poor

It is not the man who has too little, but the man who craves more, that is poor. What does it matter how much a man has laid up in his safe, or in his warehouse, how large are his flocks and how fat his dividends, if he covets his neighbor's property, and reckons, not his past gains, but his hopes of gains to come? Do you ask what is the proper limit to wealth? It is, first, to have what is necessary, and, second, to have what is enough.
Seneca

Wealth required by vanity is infinite

The wealth required by nature is limited and is easy to procure; but the wealth required by vain ideals extends to infinity.
Epicurus

Living a false purpose

Too many people go through life with a false purpose, driven either by money, social status, ego, a sense of self-worth and so on. What they do usually doesn't align with their natural inclinations or strengths so they ultimately wind up miserable and unfulfilled.
Robert Greene

(continued)

PHILOSOPHY STOLE MY AMBITION (cont'd)

Conquering the need to conquer the world

'This man has conquered the world! What have you done?' The philosopher Diogenes—the founder of Cynicism—replied without an instant's hesitation, 'I have conquered the need to conquer the world'.
Diogenes to Alexander the Great (after being told to show respect to the conqueror after having asked him to stop blocking his sun)

Desire is a sin

There is no greater sin than desire, no greater curse than discontent. *He who knows that enough is enough will always have enough.*
Lao Tzu

Or this gem ...

Life is too important to be taken seriously.
Oscar Wilde

And the knockout blow ...

Consider past times, thou shalt see the same things: some marrying, some bringing up children, some sick, some dying, some fighting, some feasting, some flattering, some boasting, some suspecting, some undermining, some wishing to die, some fretting, some wooing, some hoarding, some seeking after magistracies, and some after kingdoms. And is not that their age quite over, and ended? Again, consider now the times of Trajan. There likewise thou seest the very self-same things, and that age also is now over and ended.
Marcus Aurelius

Aurelius himself quotes a famous passage in Homer's *Iliad* that echoes this sentiment. In it, the lives of mortals are compared to leaves that grow in the spring, flourish for a season and then fall and die, only to be replaced by others.

Translation: 'Chill the f*ck out.'

You could say that I became a lot more mellow.

True to Lao Tzu's and Seneca's sentiments, I realised that I had enough. More things wouldn't make me happier. Realising this, I found a form of contentment. This had me questioning my entire approach to work and life.

A note on monocausality: It is lazy for anyone to suggest that a single X caused Y. In truth, almost all Ys are the result of a coalescence of Xs. My mellowing out was no doubt influenced by these philosophical ideas that I bought into, but also my getting older, biology, the arrival fallacy (I've made it...what now?), potential dissatisfaction with other aspects of life and myriad other factors.

But then, just like that, philosophy kindly returned my drive and ambition, with one key difference.

Finding the truth

Legendary physicist Richard Feynman said, 'We never are definitely right, we can only be sure we are wrong.' As such, I don't think that the ideas below represent the absolute truth. But they do make sense.

The following ideas funnelled my ambition away from false purposes and into meaningful pursuits aligned with my values.

The virtuous life

> Only through living virtuously can we achieve human flourishing.
> **Aristotle**

Values alignment

> Achievement of your happiness is the only moral purpose of your life, and that happiness, not pain or mindless self-indulgence, is the proof of your moral integrity, since it is the proof and the result of your loyalty to the achievement of your values.
> **Ayn Rand**

Reflecting on my values, I sought freedom from things and freedom to do things, meaningful work and time with people I care about.

(continued)

PHILOSOPHY STOLE MY AMBITION (*cont'd*)

Purpose

Making an encore appearance are the following excerpts from Marcus Aurelius' *Meditations* ...

> Nothing should be done without purpose.

> So you were born to feel 'nice'? Instead of doing things and experiencing them? Don't you see the plants, the birds, the ants and spiders and bees going about their individual tasks, putting the world in order, as best they can? And you're not willing to do your job as a human being? Why aren't you running to do what your nature demands?

Happiness

> 'Happiness' is a pointless goal ... It's all very well to think the meaning of life is happiness, but what happens when you're unhappy? Happiness is a great side effect. When it comes, accept it gratefully. But it's fleeting and unpredictable. It's not something to aim at — because it's not an aim.
> **Jordan Peterson**

These ideas gave me a sense of clarity, and helped me focus my energy and ambition on what truly matters.

Not seeking our riches to satisfy public opinion (the fallacy being that the more you have, the more people tend to resent you anyway).

It meant:

» comparing myself less

» making fewer decisions to appease other people or opinions

» less of buying 'the things' for validation

» more contentment with 'enough'

» doing work that matters instead of just seeking out money (interestingly, doing work that matters ends up making you money).

As Seneca put it, if you live according to opinion you will never be rich, but if you live according to nature, you will never be poor.

Now, it's not about just building a business that makes money. It's about building businesses that create impact. It's about sharing whatever wisdom I have attained with people who have the potential to create impact themselves.

Whether it be my writing for *Harvard Business Review*, writing [this book] or my last book, *Employee to Entrepreneur*, hosting my podcast *Future Squared*, or taking my children's entrepreneurship program, Lemonade Stand, to the world, it's all about empowering other people to be their best, but to do so in a way that is geared towards some greater purpose than simply collecting gold coins.

It also means I spend more time with family, more time with friends and more time outside of the office walls in nature, learning how to surf, hiking new spots, and…enjoying life.

If you play stupid games you win stupid prizes. Competition can blind us to what really matters, and when you take the time to reflect on what you value, as opposed to what society supposedly values, living in accordance with that changes your whole life's outlook.

Yes, philosophy stole my ambition…to make lots of money, compare myself no end and never be content, no matter how much I achieved. But it redirected that ambition into doing meaningful work, enjoying life's pleasures and living a life true to myself.

Like a philosopher is thought to have said before me, I have conquered the need to conquer the world.

APPENDIX

The 'How to run a shorter workday' experiment

The idea of running a shorter workday may sound compelling, but most think it impossible, and those who think it possible aren't clear as to how the logistics might work.

Apart from applying the previously mentioned enablers, there are some things you can do to increase your chances of successfully making the transition.

I should caveat the following by saying that six hours is arbitrary. What matters is outcomes. Running a 9-to-3 day won't necessarily be better for night owls who prefer to start working in the afternoon. Nor will it be better if that six hours is full of insecurity work like meetings and clearing our inboxes. What matters is *outcomes*.

Learnings from our 6-Hour Workday experiment

We devised an experiment based on our hypothesis that working shorter hours would not compromise productivity.

1. **Set metrics and expectations.**
   Oft-quoted management thinker Peter Drucker said that if you can measure it, you can manage it. It's not enough to

switch to shorter workdays and simply use people's opinions and your own observations, after the fact, as to whether or not people were productive. People's perceptions are subjective, and when it comes to organisational performance, we want to get to the objective.

First, define what you want to measure.

We didn't only want to measure productivity at Collective Campus, but emotional wellbeing, energy and morale.

2. **Define how you'll measure metrics.**

Use SMART metrics that you can compare to previous periods.

Our experiment was not a completely isolated scientific experiment by any stretch of the imagination. For example, I had just returned from a week away, so my general energy and wellness numbers may have been impacted accordingly. Similarly, one of my colleagues was on the fund-raising trail, which means an uphill slog and can sometimes mean hearing 'no' nine times for every single 'yes'. People say one thing but do another, which adversely impacted his energy and wellness numbers — something he admitted to.

This is why you'd want to run an initial experiment for a long enough period of time to help correct for variable external factors, and normalise the data.

As an aside, watch out for false positives and false negatives.

So, how do you measure productivity?

Performance in some roles is more measurable than in others.

Performance in a sales role, for example, is easier to quantify. You might use standard metrics such as leads generated, qualified leads, emails, phone calls made, meetings, proposals sent, follow-ups made, deals closed, the total value of deals, and so on.

These are all easily quantifiable metrics for which numerous CRM tools and app integrations exist to make your job easy.

However, for roles where the nature of the work is a little less quantifiable, we can borrow from the world of agile project management and apply what's known as story points.

Agile story points

Story points are abstract estimates of effort required to complete a task.

They are usually numbered in accordance with the Fibonacci sequence: 0, 1, 1, 2, 3, 5, 8, 13, 21, 34.

The sequence was named after the talented Middle-Ages Italian mathematician. The Fibonacci numbers are not a random set of numbers, but a phenomenon of nature. The numbers show up in pine-cones, tree branches, fruits and vegetables, shells, spiral galaxies, hurricanes, animal bodies, the uterus and DNA molecules.

For example, DNA molecules measure 34 angstroms long by 21 angstroms wide for each full cycle of their double helix spiral. These numbers, 34 and 21, are numbers in the Fibonacci series, and their ratio, 1.6190476, closely approximates Phi, which is 1.6180339.

Okay Poindexter...back to base.

To simplify, you'll observe that each successive number is obtained by adding the two previous numbers in the sequence.

Once you've determined baselines based on past performance of similar tasks, you can determine roughly how many story points particular jobs require. You'll determine what the average daily, weekly or monthly cadence is by way of total story points per person or team.

Story point sizing is relative. A story that is assigned two story points should be twice as much as a story that is assigned one story point. It should also be two-thirds of a story that is estimated three story points. When estimating story points, start with the smallest task and then score the others relative to it. See an example in figure A.1 (overleaf).

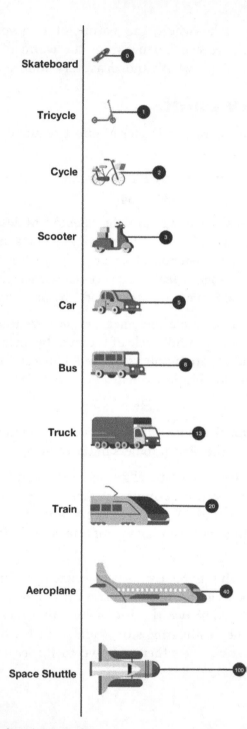

Figure A.1: agile story points

When estimating story points, you'll want to take into account:

- baseline of similar work
- amount of work
- complexity
- risks and uncertainty
- time.

Your experiment will be helped along if people record their metrics on a daily basis. In our case, it was a matter of tracking numbers and answering questions at the end and start of each day. And again, this requires a healthy degree of trust.

Our designer, Charity, used story points to determine, based on a quick review of tasks, that she had performed in the previous three months, what her average daily and weekly cadence is. She used this as her baseline to help compare and determine whether a shorter workday, with more intense focus, impacted her productivity. If it did, then her average story points completed would show a decrease.

After the experiment

I took the time to review the statistics pertaining to people's individual objective performance metrics. It's pointless running the experiment if you don't check in on the numbers.

Combine with the qualified

I distributed a Typeform survey to the team that posed the following questions to combine the quantified with the qualified and help me make data-informed decisions, as opposed to just data-driven decisions.

This gave me a better sense for more subjective matters, which would give me a better sense for whether or not the experiment validated the original hypothesis.

- How did I feel at the end of the day? Could I give more? How much more?
- How did I feel at the start of the day? Was I full of energy? Motivated?

- How did I feel during the day? Was I more focused and productive, more effective? Was the intensity too much? Did it create anxiety? Did I feel rushed?
- Did I feel like I was moving the needle towards or compromising our goals?
- Did I feel comfortable doing this? Was I waiting for others to leave first?
- What else would I like to experiment with?
- What might my ideal be?
- Do I feel like I'm falling behind my workload and have to make it up somewhere?

Team debrief

Our team met for a 30-minute meeting to review the results of the survey, the performance statistics and also to engage in a discussion about people's experiences. What did they like about the experiment? What did they *not* like? What could have been better? What were some of the challenges encountered? This works well if you have a culture of transparency where people at all levels are not afraid to speak their minds.

Our results and learnings

The entire team seemed to enjoy the experiment, and said that despite some teething issues, they maintained their usual level of quality output, deliberately spent more time in flow and felt much better in the morning. They also had more time to explore other pursuits such as dancing, yoga and, in one case, being a father to a six month old.

Statistics

The team's statistics showed no noticeable negative effect on output.

For example, my colleague Charity, the designer/marketer I introduced earlier, had no issues hitting the 50 story points that she had maintained as a daily average before diving into the experiment.

My colleague Shay, who spends most of his time on business development, managed to generate more leads during the experiment than an average week, with a flow-on effect on new opportunities created, proposals sent and sales closed, echoing the performance paradox introduced earlier.

Ultimately, we all performed just as well as we had been for the three months leading up to the experiment, except we felt much better doing it.

The one anomaly was my colleague Sean, who was engaged in a six-month capital-raising engagement for a blockchain-based spinoff. Echoing points made earlier in this book, capital raising was something that he had no experience in — it was not aligned with his strengths, something he didn't particularly enjoy and something that had a very long feedback loop. So it's no surprise to read that his general level of emotional wellbeing was around a 5.

Other learnings

As is often the case when you enter uncharted territories, you experience and learn a lot that you hadn't anticipated. We took the following additional learnings out of the experiment. You might find them valuable.

1. Break up your day

An afternoon break works wonders. One day, I worked from 9 am through to 3 pm, and made my way to the gym for a late-afternoon workout. This shot of energy inspired me to return to my laptop to crank out another two hours of what was way more productive, deep work between 5 pm and 7 pm than if I had just pushed through to 5 pm. I didn't crank out that work because I had to, but because I wanted to.

2. Capacity, outcomes and urgency (COU)

For our experiment, we determined that whether or not we called it a day at 3 pm should be contingent on three things: cognitive capacity, outcomes delivered and urgency.

Capacity

If for whatever reason, you haven't spent more than an hour in flow during the day, chances are, you've still got more to give. Give it. To do otherwise would be shortchanging your team and the mission of the organisation.

Outcomes

This book is all about a transition to an outcome-focused workplace. If the quality and timeliness of outcomes suffer, then reconsider your approach and invest the additional time required to address matters.

Urgency

You might be at capacity, but are working towards an urgent deadline the next day. In that case, it makes sense to go for a walk, go for a workout, meet a friend for a social coffee, but return to it by 4 or 5 pm so you can hit those goals. Sometimes, in business as in life, we need to dig deep and scrape the dregs of the cask to deliver—but this should be the exception rather than the rule. And if you find yourself in an organisation where you're often scraping dregs, it's an issue of not having enough resources, taking on too much work, or not using the tools and techniques introduced throughout this book.

3. It won't suit all types of work

This experiment lends itself to certain types of work, but the realities of your job may dictate that you can't just knock off at 3 pm. For example, you've got meetings scheduled at 4 pm, or perhaps you're dealing with clients in another country and the time difference means working at 9 pm. Having the flexibility to work your own hours, so long as outcomes are met, is an idea that this experiment is supposed to instil in people. Oftentimes though, you can influence externalities—such as clients and partners—so that you can move towards working the hours when you find yourself at your best.

4. Work-style preferences differ

Everybody has their own preferred work style. If you're working in a team, you've got to align individual workstyles so that they don't compromise the team's communication, collaboration and objectives. As we've learned, people have different chronotypes. Just because you're most effective at 8 am, it doesn't mean all of your colleagues will be too.

5. Avoid micromanagement

Having to track metrics on a week-to-week basis may border on micro management, and it's something I'm doing purely for the experiment. Thereafter, it's about having faith in your people not to abuse the system. Again, trust is key.

I hire people who don't need to be motivated, people who are values aligned, people who believe in what we're trying to achieve. I'm talking about self-starters who enjoy getting into flow, learning, growing as individuals and taking pride in the team's achievements.

Such experiments won't work if your people don't espouse such values, watch the clock and want to do as little work as possible. If your organisation is all about two-hour meetings with 10 people around the table because it means not actually having to think and do any real work, then a six-hour workday probably won't work for you.

6. 3 pm is a guideline, not a rule

Finishing at 3 pm is just a guideline, not a rule. In some cases, people opted to work until well after 3 pm because they were immersed in an enjoyable activity, felt they could give a little more or were working on something urgent.

7. A week is too short

What you do one week might differ considerably from what you do the next, so running the experiment over a longer period of time makes sense. But only continue running it if you're not seeing a marked drop-off in people's productivity, morale and wellness.

8. *Save rudimentary tasks for the end of the day*

If you must work beyond 3 pm, and if your cognition is maxed out by 3 pm, perhaps save rudimentary, mind-numbing tasks for the end of the day. If you can get away with it, outsource such tasks.

9. *Not for the faint-hearted*

Finally, this experiment only works with motivated people who get into flow, are outcome focused and don't normalise the 9-to-3 workday to the point where it has all the hallmarks of a standard 9-to-5 day, complete with long lunches and afternoon slumps. It can actually be painful, initially, to transition to the psyche required to successfully work only four, five or six hours a day. This is especially true if you're used to long, boozy lunches, 60-minute meetings, numerous watercooler conversations and spending half your day in transit.

A six-hour workday requires a healthy relationship with your work.

Our experiment, as such, wasn't conclusive, but it did move us towards being much less wrong about how we work.

Index